I AM THE MANIFESTER

The power lies within,
it's up to you to manifest love,
wealth and well-being.

By Tobi Ellison

TOBE ELLISON PRESS

The author and those associated with him, shall not be liable or responsible for any damage or injury allegedly arising from the methods, formulas or information put forth in this book. This book is a self-help and inspirational guide for personal development. We assume no responsibility for inaccuracies or omissions.

No part of this book may be produced commercially either by off-set printing, digital printing or on the internet without the permission of the publisher.

I Am The Manifester copyright © 2011 by Tobi Ellison
Published by ToBe Ellison,
an imprint of All About Manifesting

ISBN 978-0615495002

First Printing

www.iamthemanifester.com

ToBe Ellison Press

*Big thanks to the one woman in the world who
I love more than life itself,
Donnie Gary my beloved mother.
With great pride I move fearlessly through the world. What better gift is there than an
opportunity to dream, to create, to manifest,
to be…? I love you forever.*

*To Taylor Barnes for your lighthearted approach
to this process, and making manifesting more
enjoyable…*

*Thanks to everyone
for sharing your stories and inspiring others to
dream of the life they wish to experience.*

*Paul Kerzner you truly are a wonderful
reminder and an inspiration.*

*Su Sides thank you for your support
and encouragement.
Thank you Su for holding the vision on the days I couldn't…
"Mrs. Su from Alabama."*

*I would also like to thank all those who played a part in the manifesting, knowingly or unknowingly, of this book. Thank you all, for without your participation this would
not have been possible.*

Table of Contents

PREFACE
I

INTRODUCTION
III

MANIFESTING FORMULA DEFINED
1

PART 1
MANIFESTING STORIES
11

JEFFREY HAS A DREAM
I am manifesting at every age
12

THE APPRENTICE
I love what I love
18

CUSTOM COMFORTER
Beauty is in the eye of beholder
20

MY GREEN GUITAR
Holding onto a dream
22

SPIRAL CIRCLE
The thing I am seeking is seeking me
24

Table of Contents

HEART-CENTERED SPEAKERS
What I have to offer the world
26

COMFORTABLE SHOES
I prefer sandals
28

KNOWING MY WORTH
The world gives me what I expect
33

MY SECOND JOB
Doing what it takes
34

DELICIOUS DESSERTS
Completely in the moment
35

WORKING AT THE LAST MINUTE
Listening to my gut
37

ALL IN THE NAME OF FUN
Jokes are creative
38

SELF-ACCEPTANCE
A beautiful reminder
41

THE PERFECT TABLE
Timing is everything
43

Table of Contents

HARDWOOD FLOORS AND A FIREPLACE
Words have power
45

MY MENTAL SHOPPING LIST
Ask and you shall receive
46

THE PERFECT VACATION
Growing apart
48

MY DREAM JOB
Doing what I love
50

ROUND OTTOMAN
I want what I want
54

THERE IS NO SUCH THING AS AN ACCIDENT
There are not accidents, I should know
58

LAKERS FAN
Fond memories
63

MANIFESTED JACKET
It was meant to be
65

SEEING BEYOND THE ILLUSION
Blind faith
66

Table of Contents

A Perfect Smile
Finding a dentist
67

A Visit to California
Manifesting the money I need
68

A Big Favor
I trust that all is well
71

We Need a Vacation
Our Miami trip
72

Who Murdered My Sister?
I hear you
75

A Trip To The Post Office
I need to buy stamps
81

I Know What I Know
Everytime I...
83

The Eleventh Hour
The universe has impeccable timing.
85

Makeover
Linen pants
87

Table of Contents

ASK AND YOU SHALL RECEIVE
Sewing Machine
89

HARMONIOUS HOME
Right sized plants
91

I LOVE WHAT I DO
Taking pride in my work
93

FEARLESS FAITH
I am unstoppable
96

WE LOVE ENTERTAINING
Party planner
99

GRACIOUS LIVING
Love at first sight happens more times than not
101

I HEALED MYSELF
Laughter is the best medicine
104

THE BIG APPLE
Window shopping
106

Table of Contents

PART II

MANIFESTING PROCESS
109

EXAMPLES OF THE MANIFESTING PROCESS IN ACTION
111

MANIFESTING PROCESS FOR LOVE
112

MANIFESTING PROCESS FOR PEACE
119

MANIFESTING PROCESS FOR MONEY
124

MANIFESTING PROCESS FOR WELL-BEING
132

MANIFESTING PROCESS FOR JOY
138

PART III

AFFIRMATIONS
143

Preface

I am now consciously aware of an amazing power flowing through me. This force brings forth any and everything I am giving my attention to . . . This is happening in every moment of every day, because I am thinking of one thing or another, whether I am worried, dreaming, complaining, or even judging. Mix this train of thinking with my emotions, and it will soon show up in my experience. When I take the stance of "knowing" how a thing or a person will be, I block the miracle of the powers that be, because I have just stated my intention by my attention to what has happened in the past or what might happen in the future.

Some refer to this as the law of attraction, as karma, as reaping what you sow, as what goes around comes around. There are many ways to put words to this wondrous relationship that we all have with the vast universe. I have come to realize that this energy force is flowing through me,—in my thinking, my feeling and my words. Put this together, and you get one powerful manifester!

I am not offering you anything you don't already possess. What I am offering you is an opportunity to live the life of your dreams. You'll notice that in the stories everyone is thinking something different, but their basic needs are the same: love, happiness, well-being, and financial security. These things are manifested in countless ways, for each Individual sees his or her world differently. It is when we stand In judgment we start to concern ourselves with what others are doing and how they might use this power, their power! My desire is to remind you of this remarkable spiritual experience you can have when you make the decision to live your life as a conscious manifester.

My inspiration for writing this book came to me after my car crash. I had been feeling wonderful just before the accident, and I couldn't believe it happened to me. I wanted to know how could this have happened? I am a safe driver for goodness sake! For a moment, I questioned everything I had believed to be my truth. There was nowhere to turn. What was there to believe?

Until that moment, I believed in the power of positive thinking. I believed that we reap what we sow, and what goes around comes around and any other cliché that applies, but in that moment, I felt helpless and utterly hopeless. Where were my angels? Why didn't they prevent this from happening? Why didn't they give me a sign? When I finally got home, I retraced the thoughts that had led me to that place of fear and helplessness, and it all began to make sense.

What this did for me was confirm the power/force we use with little or no understanding. Some people want to go to school, start a family, find a new job, a lover, a husband, a wife, more money, great health, peace of mind… the list goes on forever. As you begin to understand how to use your energy, your life will begin to align with what you desire. I believe that anything less is a misuse of your power.

This Energy is continuously flowing through everything and everyone in the universe. There is no getting around it—we are endowed with this mighty force. It's in our very nature.

Don't take my word for it. Let your life experience be the example, the reminder. After careful observation, it became painfully obvious that no one was doing anything to me. I continued to find myself in the same predicaments, wondering, "Why me?" It was not until I began to ask myself the right question that I stopped playing the blame game. I wanted to know what part am I playing in manifesting these repetitive experiences. I am now willing to pay attention to what I'm focused on, to how I'm feeling. This is the beginning of becoming a conscious manifester!

May you find the courage to use your power to change and heal yourself and your world.

Introduction

I now see my world through new eyes, through the eyes of, the manifester. With this new perception, I have the power to change my world.

I used to think that things were, happening to me. I often thought I needed to wait and see what the world might serve up next. I was going about my life looking at what was, and hoping for something to change. I was clueless to the fact that I was calling it forth myself! When things were not going the way I wanted them to, I blamed it on fate, bad luck, bad timing, anything but my own deep desires. Why me? I exclaimed. I felt victimized by the world around me, by the world at large. I had no real understanding of the truth of who and what I am... the manifester!

As I began to seek a deeper level of awareness, things began to make sense. I needed to get honest with myself. I had been letting other people's opinions about me flow through my mind, and I had adopted them as my own. Although my surroundings had changed, the old music continued to play. It didn't matter where I was, or what I did; I could and often would attract the same scenario with my old train of thought.

The people around me were mirroring my own insecurities about myself—but how could they know my innermost feelings? The things I feared the most kept becoming my external experiences. My fears resided deep within awaiting the next opportunity to reveal themselves.

The more I wanted change, the less change there was. I continued to recreate the very thing I wanted to move away from. The thing I wanted to avoid. Why did I keep doing the things I most wanted to stop doing? I was soon going to learn that it was my inner world that needed to change.

Is it possible that the world was showing me the parts of myself that needed to be healed? This idea didn't sink in for a long time. I continued to

Introduction

run, meeting myself at every turn. I had internalized an unhealthy perception of self. Like so many of us, I had never questioned the lyrics of the songs that had played in the back of my mind for most of my life.

I had allowed old programming to dictate my behavior. My thinking had become undisciplined and I had wandered away from what I really wanted. I was always dwelling on the past or worried about the future, and it didn't matter whether I was thinking constructive or destructive thoughts—I was manifesting them all. It matters not in which direction we allow our thoughts to flow. If we focus long enough we will manifest feeling around these thoughts. Now we are manifesting based on the feelings we have attached to the thought. This will empower the thoughts and make them manifest more quickly in our experience. It works both ways what we want and the things we say we don't want.

When I am happy, I manifest happy experiences with the joy I feel, and my joy attracts joyful people. The same is true when I am feeling depressed, angry or off-balance. We only notice things similar to the way we feel. The more we notice, the more there is to notice around us in either direction, your life will be filled with joy or despair. We can choose to see through eyes of love or fear.

Two useful phrases comes to mind:

Fake it till you make it.
and
Act as if.

I know that manifesting is a process. We manifest experiences constantly, with or without our conscious participation. If we know what we are seeking, we can manifest intentionally. Know thyself, and you will create your desires.

When I am manifesting, I am at ease with myself and I am feeling clear about my desire. I am free of judgment and in complete appreciation of all that I have. It doesn't matter what I'm focused on—whatever it is, it will simply be. If I'm fearful, I'm manifesting just as powerfully as when I'm confident or blissful.

Judgment is a powerful tool, and is often times turned against me. When I stand in judgment of others, I immediately create limitations to what my own heart and mind can manifest—I get more of the things I don't want. All the jokes and judgments I've made at another's expense lived inside me, reminding me of my own insecurities.

Do unto others as you would have them do unto you.

These words began to make themselves more known on a daily basis. Case in point this day would change my life forever, it came full circle. I would have to make a choice! I would have to decide whether I wanted to continue to live a life of fear or choose a life of love. If I were to choose a life of fear, I could continue on the path of disconnectedness, and I could pretend that I wasn't hearing the disempowering words and warning signs I had gotten about a person or situation, only to say later, "Something told me..." "I had a feeling!"– sound familiar?

I was working in a clothing store in West Hollywood, California, where I was required to wear an article of the designer's clothing every day. The clothes were very fitted and left little to the imagination, and on this particular day, I was feeling bold. I decided to wear a complete outfit: a matching shirt and pants, all in brown, complete with matching shoes and belt. I must have looked like a big Tootsie Roll in my cat suit, but at the time I thought I was a sight to behold.

I lived in a humble and rather conservative Mexican neighborhood on the Far East side of Los Angeles, where the concept of noise ordinance was nonexistent. My neighbors had a party almost every week with music so loud I could feel it vibrating my feet as I walked around my apartment, but I never thought to ask them to turn it down. There was always something going on. People were hanging out in the courtyard. The neighbors across the hall often had their front door open. It seemed like a frat house. There were at least five or six men living in a one-bedroom apartment across the hall from me. Once when I came home, one of the guys across the hall walked out to meet me. He walked directly behind me and tried to follow me into my apartment, saying, in broken English, "I hear you chanting *nam myo ho renge kyo*," repeating the Buddhist chant I used during meditation. The guys watched and waited for my response and eventually called him back home. It was obvious that he had been drinking. Aside from incidences like that, it was an okay place to live.

I was comfortable in my cat suit once I was at work in West Hollywood, where the most outrageous outfits wouldn't cause an eyelash to bat. But sud-

Introduction

denly, I wasn't comfortable walking out of my apartment; I didn't want to be judged by the standards of my neighbors. It became an obstacle course just to leave my home. I needed to walk out of my upstairs apartment and get past my neighbor across the hall and the two below me on both sides of the stairwell. Once past them, I had to walk through the courtyard to my car. I had to open the gate, back out in my car, close the gate, and then finally I was off to work. While I was actually getting dressed, none of this crossed my mind. But right before I walked out the door, it hit me: I couldn't do it! I couldn't open the door. I stood there frozen. Thoughts began to flood my mind; I didn't want to be judged.

The power of the word and the power I had given the word is my lesson here. I knew that I was not comfortable wearing the cat suit in certain environments. Now I was confronted with a dilemma. Truthfully, if I'd had more time I would have changed my clothes, but instead I had to make a decision, and quickly.

I was standing at the front door in my brown cat suit. I hesitated—I couldn't open the door. I couldn't do it. "What's wrong with you? Why can't you walk out this door?" Fears started to rise from deep within me, awakened by my insecurities. As I backed away from my front door, the words came flowing through me and the feelings of being judged were front and center. I made my way to the bathroom to have one last look at myself. I looked into my eyes and asked, "What's wrong with you? Why can't you walk out the door?" Before I could finish, my answer came forth. "I don't want to be judged. I don't want someone to make catcalls. Why can't you wear this?" As I stood there repeating the question, I could feel a wave of energy in the form of thoughts and feelings simultaneously caress me with the answer. "You haven't given yourself permission."

In that moment, I could sense that the only person whose opinion mattered most was staring back at me. Loving me just as I was—brown cat suit and all.

I was freed from the emotional shackles of my own self-judgment and fear. I had listened to my soul and believed it. Within five minutes, I was out the door. Self-acceptance is what I saw in the mirror on that magical day. I had accepted myself with compassion and self-approval. It no longer mattered what anyone else thought of me. The fear of judgment was gone and had been replaced with self-love and a feeling of being carefree.

I walked confidently into my neighborhood with no concern about what someone might say. Honestly, it didn't matter. I had the approval of the most important person: me.

To my delightful surprise, there was no one in sight. It was indeed a magical moment. I calmly walked to my car with a completely different mindset. I got into my car and drove to work. When I got to West Hollywood and crossed the street to the store, a woman ran out of a hair salon to ask breathlessly, "Where did you get your outfit?" I told her about my store and pointed the way, and an hour or so later she came by to purchase the complete outfit. Beauty truly is in the eye of the beholder—on that day, I was beautiful from the inside out. It was never the clothes that needed to change, but my perception of myself. I needed to give myself permission to be me, to be fabulous, and to be whatever I wanted to be in any given moment.

Join me on this magical journey and remember the truth of who we are, and may we have the courage to live it! We are all manifesters focused in different directions. It is when we mind our business do we become the powerful positive examples of this truth.

Manifesting Formula Defined

CLARITY
APPRECIATION
ALIGNMENT
ENERGETIC FOUNDATION
EXPECTANCY
WORDS AND AFFIRMATIONS
INTENTION
IMAGINATION
FEELING IT (KNOWING)
TRUST
SURRENDER (NO WORRIES)

Clarity

Get clear about your desires. What is it you want? Why do you want this thing or experience? Choose one area or thing in your life and decide. Without worrying about the how, just take a moment and dream the ideal scenario around your desires. What is it? Money, love, a relationship, new friends, a new career, a harmonious life, perfect health, peace of mind, abundance? The list can go on forever—there is no end to what is possible if you get clear about your desires.

When you are willing to imagine it without worry, fear, doubt, and the hows, you are well on your way to manifesting a new experience. Hopefully it is what you really want.

This must be something you believe is possible. If you don't believe you are deserving of the thing you wish to manifest, use affirmations to shift your thoughts until your desire becomes more attainable for you.

You must be willing to tune into the limitless possibilities of the truth of who you are, and choose to experience something new. Tell a new story around the things you wish to see manifested. Speak as if it is happening, coming from a place of truth and confidence: what is it you prefer to experience? What could you be excited about? Keep asking the right questions until you are clear.

Appreciation

Seeking the best in every situation, giving thanks for what you have and where you are—in your job, your relationship or your independence, in your home. If you truly wish to change your life, start appreciating all that you are and all you've manifested up until this moment. Remember: there is always a new and better thought available if you want it!

Is it an ideal relationship? What could you appreciate about yourself

Manifesting Formula Defined

for being in this relationship? What could you appreciate about yourself for being ready for the love you seek? What do you appreciate about being in a healthy, harmonious, romantic relationship? What are you excited about? What are you expecting?

When you are appreciating, what you manifest must be in alignment with the feelings you offer.

Once you tune into the beauty and goodness, you will have a new experience around your past and present relationships. You will look forward to love.

Appreciating must be a natural response to the thing you are admiring. If it is something you really want, this will be easy. You will ease into oneness because of your love for it. It is a natural reaction to what you wish to manifest, even if it's the perfect lover, career, promotion, home, or a state of peace and wealth. As you move into a more harmonious emotional space, you have a greater chance of manifesting the desires of your heart.

Now you should feel better. It is from this place that will bring the mate, job, house, peace of mind, perfect health, and abundance. You need only appreciate to see something new in your experience.

Alignment

The act of alignment is to get in line with your desires. What if you want a new car—what are some ways that you could get aligned with it? Tune in first to the style, color, size, and price range of the car you want. Once you have decided on something, the ideas will begin to flow. It happens naturally. This is alignment. When you think of an object or an experience, you first get the thought, then ideas follow that tell you what you might need to do next. I offer this process so that you may make a conscious effort with a clear understanding of how you have gotten the things you have in your life. You can also align with a state of being.

Energetic Foundation

Consume yourself with your desire until it's clear that you must have it in your being and your feeling space. What this means is that you are no longer looking for the thing you've asked for. You are at ease, at peace with your wish. It is apparent that the thing you want is making its way into your experience. All things are created from this place. This is the absolute truth, for you are the manifester. Another way of looking at energetic foundation is to understand that you are no longer distracted by outside illusion in situations. It is knowingness, from the inside out. A feeling of peace and calm assures you that all is well when you have replaced your feelings of worry, doubt, and fear. You are now open to all possible avenues from which your desire may come.

There is no time limit on the process. Your power is always in the present moment. No one and nothing can deter you from manifesting what you say you want. This harmonious enthusiasm becomes a part of your energetic foundation. You are standing on solid ground, fearlessly moving through life in peace.

Expectancy

Expectancy is the act or state of expecting. What is it that you are expecting? Truth be told, you always get what you expect. I'm sure you know this intellectually, but do you comprehend the concept? How often do you think about what you're expecting? If you are willing to take the time to sit with yourself for a moment and reflect on what you are now experiencing, what part of it did you expect? Be honest. Take another look at your life.

If you have a week to repay a debt, what will you prepare for? Are you going to imagine yourself meeting your obligation on time? Will you come up with some excuse about why you need more time? It matters not what you choose— you are right either way. You are either expecting to have the debt paid on time or you are not; it is that simple. In that moment, people decide on the path they believe is most possible.

When you are aligned with the thing you are expecting, your behavior follows naturally. If you want to know what you expect in your life or what you have been expecting, look at your life with an open heart, through eyes of love and compassion. How about this: are you expecting to meet the love of your life? Are you expecting to live an abundant life? If you are, what are you doing on a daily basis to experience the thing you're expecting?

Are you excited about life? Are you greeting the day with hope and optimism? You must expect things to go well. It doesn't matter if it's the life you've imagined or the one you're trying to avoid; you will get what you expect.

Words and Affirmations

Words are very powerful! Our lack of awareness of this power holds us captive in our misery. We misuse our power; by turning it against ourselves, we are creating the very thing we fear most.

Use your words to help get clarity, to get into alignment. You can talk yourself into believing almost anything. Do you not find this to be the truth when you're listening to the media? Why not choose something worth talking about? Why not talk about things you wish to manifest? Words are faithful servants, forever bringing forth the ideas to which they have been matched. We are constantly talking ourselves into all sorts of conditions. Be willing to use your words to heal, inspire and to encourage.

I remember suggesting this to a friend about a mutual friend with whom

I was doing life coaching. I mentioned the excitement of working with this individual. He took it upon himself to give his unflattering opinion of her. I responded, "Why not share the good news? Why not talk about her being positive, lighthearted, funny, and willing to be better?" Without missing a beat, he responded, "I need to say these things to myself first." No words could have been truer; you cannot give what you do not have. Choose your words with careful consideration, using them as the powerful tools for which they are intended, to change your life for the better.

But don't take my word for it—no pun intended. Look at your life. What do you speak of most? Notice the correlation between the things you share and your experience. It must be one of two things: a life of love or a life of fear. A life of lack or abundance. A life of fun or an uphill battle. The universe takes you at your word. It is not trying to problem-solve for you. It could care less about this or that statement; it's up to you to mean what you say and say what you mean.

INTENTION

Intention is a determination to act in a certain way. What do you intend to do to manifest your desires? For starters, you could intend to use the formula to manifest your desires. What more is there than to manifest a life worth living by your own standards? You could intend to pay attention to your thoughts, intend to shift your thinking. How about telling a new story? One you wish to experience?

Are you intending to live the life of your dreams? Do you intend to live an abundant life? What about intending to be happy, at peace, a better person, a better parent, husband, wife, friend, lover, brother, uncle, sister, employer, employee? Consider being a better example; why not intend to discover this truth for yourself!

This concept to me means having clarity about something I desire to experience or manifest. How often do you intend to have a nice day? Do you intend to live happily ever after?

Remember: you are intending a life filled with love, magic and beauty! You are in the driver's seat—you are consciously participating in the manifesting process, and so it is…

IMAGINATION

Is the act or power to form a mental Image of something that is not present. Which images come to mind when you think of your desires? The thing or experience you wish to imagine must be something that you believe is possible. The life you are now living is the one you have given thought to; you gave it so much thought, in fact, you brought it into your experience. It is either the thing you wanted or the thing you are complaining about not wanting. It doesn't matter if you're dreaming, reminiscing, storytelling or fantasizing—all invoke the imagination. In any of these states, you will call forth images similar to what you are giving your attention to. May you imagine something worthwhile!

The question then arises, what's real? It's a known fact that the subconscious mind can't tell the difference between what's real or imagined. What a wonderful gift! No one has power over what we think unless we give it to them. You can imagine anything under the moon—if you believe it without a shadow of a doubt, then it will be made manifest. Why not sit with yourself and imagine things working out in your favor? Imagine a better job, more money, better health, a new car. It's your imagination; use it wisely. Whatever the mind can perceive and you believe, you will achieve.

If I can imagine something with feeling, and put all of my senses to work, then I can manifest it. How does it feel? What does it look like? What do you hear? Can you taste it? If you are willing to put forth the effort to imagine something more, you can manifest your desire.

Feeling It

Sensation is experienced through the senses. How are you feeling about the thing you wish to manifest?

Are you worried, or do you believe all is well? Both perceptions will bring about feelings. One will be harmonious, the other, inharmonious. The trick is knowing the difference. I know it sounds silly that one would not choose the better feelings, but believe it or not, some of us are conditioned to accept certain feeling states as the norm. One would think that most people would reach for the better-feeling state of being, but that's not necessarily true, especially if you have lived in a negative, inharmonious energetic space.

Case in point: a lot of people enjoyed watching Jerry Springer's talk show, in the name of entertainment. I must admit, I have watched a time or two! Some of the topics were so ridiculous that I thought the show had to be staged, but this didn't stop me from experiencing sadness while wanting to distract myself from myself.

You notice your world from where you reside emotionally. If you are not happy, you will notice all the unhappy things in the world. Your topic of conversation reflects the way you feel. The people you attract feel similar to you. The music you listen to, the movies you watch—everything you surround yourself with is an exact match to the way you're feeling. Like attracts like. Talk about being a bearer of bad news—or as I like to say, Bad News Betty! This is because you are feeling it; you are offering emotions around unhappiness.

Consider thinking a new thought and offering better feelings. I assure you, your world will soon respond to what you are feeling about your circumstances. Remember to **"Act as if,"** and you'll feel your way to a better state of being, a better life, a better you.

TRUST

Trust is the firm reliance on the integrity, ability or character of a person or thing. Know that what you desire is done, even if you don't have it in your experience. When you trust, you behave in a confident manner.

Trust can only come from within. If you haven't cultivated a healthy relationship with yourself, you will have trust issues. It is never about not trusting someone else. Once you truly trust yourself, the rest is easy. That connection is always there—it is up to you to understand it, to know that the truth is inside you, wanting to give you the answers you desire.

We allow other voices to drown out our own and then blame others for not trusting or listening to ourselves. If we are preoccupied with the outside world, we will not know who to trust, and we won't be able to hear our truth. We can't know which voice or feeling to trust if we aren't paying attention to our own.

To trust is believing in the unseen and doing it anyway. It is worth the risk. But it's true that most would prefer to see the path.

SURRENDER

To surrender is to give over, resign, or go with the flow, to release your desires to the universe.

I know from experience that the universe has impeccable timing and taste. It is up to you to let go and leave the wonderful details to the master. Let the universe move heaven and earth to bring you the desires of your heart!

When you truly surrender, you are not talking about your desire from a place of "where is it?" There is no worrying in true surrender. Just simply allow it to make itself known in your physical experience. You will forget about it, and before long, you will see signs leading you to your wish.

If you need something immediately, shift your energy, everything depends upon your complete surrender to the belief, the knowing that it is done. As you read these stories, you will see examples of timing and how things happen at just the right moments. The people in these stories were appreciating, trusting, and using words and affirmations; they were feeling the thing they wanted. They were in alignment with their desires. With clarity, imagination, expectancy, and intention, they were standing on an energetic foundation in total surrender. Now what are you willing to manifest?

part one
Manifesting Stories

Jeffrey Has A Dream
I am manifesting at every age

*My words are made manifest
by my beliefs and intentions.*

Manifesting is simple. In fact, it is so simple that even a thirteen-year-old boy can do it.

Jeffrey is a typical thirteen-year-old with a passion for rock music. The only thing that he thought he needed to complete himself was a black and white, totally cool Warlock guitar. His room was covered with pictures of the guitar, he would listen to musicians who played that guitar and he spent hours playing air guitar. Jeffrey was manifesting the guitar of his dreams, but he didn't know it. All he needed was a little guidance.

Jeffrey and I discussed his desire to own this guitar, but his emotions around how he would get it were self-defeating and reflected a feeling of unworthiness. I said to Jeffrey, "You can have anything you want."

He said, "What do you mean?"

I said, "Let's play a game. Think of something you want. The rules of the game are, you cannot worry about the money. It is about focusing on the thing you are wanting. Now name something you want, and let's make a reasonable time frame in which to get it."

Jeffrey immediately said, "I want a Warlock guitar! But it's five hundred dollars."

I reminded him again that he couldn't worry about the money or where it's going to come from. In the spirit of trying to positively encourage him, I suggested all the ways the money could come to him. I mentioned doing chores around the house, mowing lawns for the neighbors, borrowing it from his mother or his grandmother, but he dismissed all of these options with seemingly valid excuses.

I realized I had to divert his attention from the impossibility to the possibility. I said, "Let's choose a time frame which is realistic for you to manifest this guitar." Jeffrey decided upon his birthday, which was about three months away.

Following are the emails Jeffrey and I wrote to each other as he played the manifesting game. His willingness to play along was sweet, but I knew it wasn't a game. I was tempted to help buy the guitar for him, but I knew it would defeat the purpose: to teach him that he had all he needed within him to manifest this guitar on his own.

August 6

Jeffrey: Hey, it's Jeff. Hey, I was just wondering, how am I gonna get the Warlock if I don't worry about the money? But I guess I'll just keep up with what you told me. I got a lot of pics of it and even my girlfriend got a new red Warlock. You do know which one it is, right? Yeah well, I'm getting more excited, because August 30 is right around the corner. I'm just dropping by to say what's up and see how your writing was going, so when you get this, write back if you can.

Me: Hello, I am excited for you! Jeff, it is a very simple process. Remember when you were younger and you were asked what you wanted for your birthday? The person asking was willing to give you whatever you wanted. In that moment, when they asked, "What do you want?" your thoughts raced back and forth across the history of all you had seen and thought. "Maybe I want a video game or a skateboard." In fact, what you were doing was preparing for one of the things you had noticed before you were asked the question that you knew would be coming. When the time came, when the question was asked, you were ready. You blurted out the thing and knew the gift would be on its way. The person asking the question was someone you trust, and you knew they would keep their promise. My point is, you were not worried about the money. You knew the gift would be in your possession very soon. You may have told a few friends about what you were expecting to get. Jeff, start giving thanks for your Warlock guitar. The stronger your belief, the more real it feels, and the sooner your Warlock guitar will be in your hands. Go to your girlfriend's and practice with her. Imagine the two of you playing together. Take turns playing the guitar—while one is holding the red guitar, the other person imagines playing the tribal one. Jeff, make this experience real—know it! And soon the experience will be a reality.

August 7

Jeffrey: Hey yeah, I've gotten really excited since August started, and the whole thing with the going to the girlfriend's house, I can't do, because her parents hate me, like really bad. I'm not even supposed to be talking to her, but we do every night anyway. But yeah, I guess I'll think about what you said. And I wanna thank you.

Me: I am sorry to hear that. I hope you continue to imagine having your Warlock guitar. It will come. It is your belief that will make the difference.

August 8

Jeffrey: Don't worry, I'm believing all right, like the most I ever have before. Every day when I listen to my music, I picture myself as Munky (rhythm guitarist for KoRn). I always got them playing. Now it's hard not to believe with the Warlock. Thank you again.

Me: Good work, my friend.

August 31

Me: Hello, how are you? Are you as excited today as you were last week? I hope you are more excited. Jeff, trust and expect your guitar to show up. Start giving thanks now! Believe, and so shall it be.

September 20

Me: Hello! I hope you are preparing for your guitar. I watched an amazing movie about the very thing we have been talking about. The movie is The Secret. It is incredible. You can order it online for $4.99—it's a must-see. Ask your mother if need be to order it. It will encourage you that much more. Let me know what you think.

September 21

Jeffrey: Just a thought—how am I gonna get it? I thought I was gonna get it the 30th or in August? But yeah, I'll look into it. There's a lot of new stuff I listen to and watch and whatnot, like Slipknot and stuff. But yeah, I was like really excited and whatnot, like I was sort of jumpy that week and all my friends sort of noticed, and I told them, too, and I was supposed to go to a KoRn concert the 20th at 7 in West Palm and then stay at Uncle Greg's house and stay the night, but my friend's parents said no, so I couldn't go cuz Uncle Greg didn't want me to go alone cuz it was just gonna be me and Anthonie. But yeah, that's how it's been around here. I can't really hold in all this anticipation any more, man.

Me: I will hold it for you, my friend. I want you to watch the movie The Secret. I believe in you and I am telling you, it's the law of the land. It can't not happen. Your imagination is all you have. It's up to you to use it. When you are looking for the movie, look for Ester Hicks' name, then choose that site. I know you are sharp enough to follow it. Keep the energy flowing—it will happen.

SEPTEMBER 22

Me: Google The Secret, count three sites down, and watch the trailer.

From Jeffrey: Could you send it to me?

Me: Sure.

From Jeffrey: Is it a movie offline? I'll try to look for it, but my mom doesn't have a credit card and my grandmother won't pay to just watch a movie online. But yeah, I'll look.

Me: It's online and it is $4.95. I believe it will be very helpful.

SEPTEMBER 23

From Jeffrey: I saw the preview. I'll have to ask my grandmother if I can use her credit card to buy it.

Me: You could watch it on the Internet for five dollars, what do you think? I think it's everything you and I have been doing. Now you will hear it from others who have put it to the test.

From Jeffrey: I know its five dollars, but I gotta get my grandmother to let me get it with her credit card.

Me: Good luck.

OCTOBER 16TH

From Jeffrey: Hey Ellison, I'm getting my guitar! It should be here by the 18th. You told me to be determined to get it, so I just didn't give up. I sort of bugged Uncle Greg for it for my b-day, and he got it for me. Write back sometime.

Me: I knew you would get it! I did consider asking your uncle, but I knew it had to come from you. I thought to call you to have you ask for it for your birthday. I am so excited for you! With the same determination, use your power of attraction to manifest the best you can imagine.

Jeffrey employed his imagination by putting images all over his room and pretending he was in a rock band. He needed to use affirmations to shift his energy. He needed to trust and surrender the idea of how the mon-

ey would come. Every time Jeffrey was distracted, I happily reminded him of his intention. I had him focus on his guitar, and he believed the guitar would come. It was the innocence of a child that allowed Jeffrey to trust me and surrender his fears so that he could focus on the end result.

The Apprentice
I love what I love

*The desires of my heart continue
to flow through me and to me.*

I've always had a natural talent for putting together a home. Even as a kid, I used to rearrange the furniture on a biweekly basis, much to the concern of my mother. I knew I had a special skill; I could visualize the most random items and create magical spaces for people to live in—and do it on a shoestring budget. This ability to creatively give to others worked best when I listened to people's needs and fulfilled them. I had a desire to be of service to people in interior design.

Unfortunately, my talents in this area were thwarted until much later. When they reemerged, I began to do freelance decorating. I had learned many aspects of interior design, but I decided that I needed to learn how to do window treatments if my business was to succeed. This meant that I needed to learn to sew, so I went to a fabric store to see what they offered in the way of classes. I had collected many books on window treatments, and now I was ready to design my own. I bought a sewing machine, but I needed someone to teach me how to use it. I was looking at class schedules and showing the universe my intent to find a teacher, but time kept slipping away. I wasn't getting around to taking a class.

During this time, I was teaching workshops at a bookstore and from time-to-time using the space for readings when I needed to. One day, a woman came in seeking a reading. She had been referred to me, and after the reading, she mentioned that she'd recently started a new business. She handed me her card, and I saw that she was in the business of making window treatments. I told her I was a freelance designer as well, and she said, "Why don't you come by my store?"

I decided to visit her store, thinking that if I liked her work, maybe I would refer my clients to her. But when I walked into her little storefront design studio, I was knocked out. She had every type and texture of fabric and trim you could imagine, in the most gorgeous materials a designer could dream of. We got down to business and I made her an offer she couldn't refuse: I would work for free if she would teach me how to make window treatments as gorgeous as she made. She had been designing for over twenty years and had studied in New York at the Fashion Institute of Technology—I could not have asked for a better teacher! Within a week, I was in her garage learning how to put panels together.

Talk about perfect timing! I set out to take a class in sewing, and now I had a top-notch designer of window treatments teaching me. I had an intent to learn to sew, which implied that I wanted a teacher. My teacher could have been anyone, but because I put no restrictions on how I wanted to learn this skill, the universe sent me the perfect teacher.

I now understand the phrase "Before you ask, it is given." It was on its way the moment I gave thought to it. Now that's powerful! I must be willing to dream a new dream, tell a new story and let the universe handle the details. Not only did I learn to make window treatments, but I did it with a highly trained professional in the privacy of her home. I could not have paid for such an experience. It was truly more than I had anticipated. With encounters like this, why wouldn't I trust the universe for all of my needs?

appreciation

Custom Comforter
Beauty is in the eyes of the beholder

I appreciate all I love and
my world responds with magic and precision.

I was working in an interior design studio learning how to make window treatments and bedding and work with upholstery, when I saw a magazine picture of the most perfect bedroom I had ever seen. I was immediately transported to that place. The focal point of the room was a gorgeous comforter on the bed. It was a perfect square with inverted pleats that was absolutely stunning. You have NO IDEA how much I loved that comforter!

I shared this vision with the woman I was working with, but she couldn't have cared less. I sat admiring the picture for a while longer and then put it aside. Later that day I received a phone call from a dear friend, inviting me over the next day. I always loved visiting her; she is a spiritual medium with a wild sense of humor—we always had a great time.

When I arrived at my friend's, she said, "Oh, I have something for you!" She was always trying to give me stuff, and it was always something cute, so I was excited to see what this gift would be. She went upstairs and came down with a large, clear bedding bag. I recognized the fabric immediately—it was the comforter I had been admiring in the magazine photo, but a different color, same design with inverted pleats and all! I screamed, "Are you sure, are you sure you want me to have this?"

When I walked away with my beautiful comforter under my arm, I realized that I was in full alignment with the power of appreciation. The image of the comforter, which had conjured up such amazing feelings within me, had now manifested itself in my life.

In every moment, we are creating. The better we feel, the more harmonious our lives will be. The universe is always giving us the things we are giving our attention to. I am now choosing to notice the things I wish to experience.

I see my life unfolding in the most amazing ways. The more I continue to see what I desire to experience, the more experience and fulfilling a life I manifest for myself.

The Green Guitar
Holding onto a dream

*I hold the vision, which I desire to experience,
talking about the goodness and giving thanks.*

I purchased a beautiful dark green acoustic guitar. I even took a few lessons because the instrument inspired me. One day, though, I came home to find that it had fallen off its stand and was on the floor, its neck broken.

I thought I could glue it back together, and I did. I had spoken to a few people and they thought that it was ruined; I would never be able to play it again. But I couldn't let go of it; I loved that green guitar too much. I carried it with me from place to place. Seven years later, I still had not had it re-strung.

One day, I was hanging out with a friend who plays the guitar, and I mentioned my green guitar to him. He asked if he could see it. I showed it to him, and he said he would take it by the guitar shop to ask what could be done.

Days later, my friend brought the guitar by my work place with great news. They had put new strings on it, and it worked just fine! It turns out; they would have glued it just as I did. Truthfully, I hadn't been sure whether the guitar could be repaired. I loved it and didn't want to part with it, and thank goodness I hadn't. I have that guitar to this day, because it holds the promise that I will someday be a musician.

My love for my guitar would not let me part with it. It would be seven years before I would have it working again. When I took it in for repairs, I was told it would never work again, but I couldn't part with it. Thank goodness I listened to my heart! My challenge is always to trust my feelings. On the days that I was trying to figure out what to do with my broken guitar, the thought of hanging it on the wall as a piece of art did cross my mind. One thing was for sure, I could not imagine parting with it.

The Spiral Circle
The thing I am seeking is seeking me

*The universe aligns with the desires of my heart
in every moment without question.*

At one point, I checked out some meditation videos in an attempt to teach myself to meditate, but they were of no help. If I remember correctly, there was someone standing on the beach talking about meditation with the ocean in the background. I did try it, but I was not content with the method. I decided to return them to the library.

One Friday night when I was out dancing at a club, a friend wanted to give me his new phone number. He asked me if he should write it down, and I replied, "No! I will remember it!" But when I tried to call him a few days later, the person who answered the phone told me I had the wrong number. I tried a couple more times, and the same person picked up each time, announcing, "Spiral Circle Bookstore. May I help you?" Finally I asked, "What kind of bookstore is this?" She replied, "A metaphysical bookstore." I asked, "Do you have tapes on meditation?" She said, "Do we ever!"

I got the address and made my way to a lovely blue house that was filled with all the spirituality books and tapes I could imagine, plus candles, crystals, music and more. It was heaven for me! I began that day to support the store and to this day, whenever I am in Orlando, I make my way there. I have met wonderful teachers on my journey through the Spiral Circle, and it is the place I taught my first workshop. I am grateful to Beverly, the owner, and her lovely team for being a source of inspiration when I needed it.

I am seeking spiritual understanding. The universe arranged the perfect opportunity for me to move forward on my journey. It is up to me to take the next step. I am grateful and I trust the signs from the universe. I am open to evolving, and a way is being made for me on a daily basis. I only need to trust my feelings and continue to ask for guidance.

Heart-Centered Speakers
What I have to offer the world

*The better I am, the better I will be
and the more I will have to give.*

I was seeking employment by looking through metaphysical magazines when I noticed a group for speakers who are interested in readings and mediumship. It was a forum for practicing your craft, getting feedback from audience members, and a source of advice. I thought it was a great idea. I called to get some info about the class and learned that it was held once a month and cost fifteen dollars to attend. I forget the reason I didn't jump at the chance to get there sooner.

I soon found a new job and eight months had gone by when I got an email about the next heart-centered speakers group. I thought about going; I had Wednesdays off then, whereas before I had been busy on Wednesday nights, so now I had no excuse. But it turned out that the group met two hours away from where I lived, and it made little sense to me to drive four hours for an hour-and-a-half-long meeting.

I didn't go. Within a couple of weeks of that invite, I got another email from the group, announcing that they were starting a new group in Los Angeles. I was excited now—that would be a bit closer! I read further; the next meeting was the next day, a Sunday… at my work place, the Mystic Journey bookstore. The group had come to me. I was beside myself! Needless to say, I attended the workshop. It is amazing to come to an understanding of your own part in manifesting the desires of your heart.

My desires are aligned with truth and service, flowing through me, guiding me to my next experience. I look for love in every moment. I know my prayers are being answered. I need only trust and surrender. I am always grateful for such humbling experiences. I will never tire of seeing how all I love flows to me. I offer the love of it, and it is up to the universe to decide how it will show up in my life. This is co-creation at it's best.

Comfortable Shoes
I prefer sandals

The universe is abundant
and gives abundantly.

I needed more shoes. It was raining and I had open-toed shoes on, sandals. I couldn't continue wearing sandals in this weather. I didn't want to ruin my shoes, and it was too cold anyway, by the time my workday was over. I talked with a coworker about needing new shoes and I expressed the need for a more casual shoe, something weather-appropriate for the cold and rain.

I couldn't help but long for my sandals, though. I dreaded the idea of having to look for casual shoes. I wear a lot of sandals, but they are pretty nice and pretty stylish; some are leather with straps across the top, some are more of a mule with a nice heel. I do love a nice heel; the sound is calming and sometimes even funny. When I shop for new shoes, I even walk around in circles listening to the sound of the shoe. For me, the sound of a heel can be very telling—I do know the sound of a well-made shoe. I have a pair of leather sandals that I've changed the soles on at least three times, and they still look fabulous. I have worn and re-worn those sandals out!

But now I had to put away my heels and find a more casual shoe, and I was not happy about it. I was sure I could find a casual shoe with a nice heel, but it wasn't as fun for me. I do have a nice pair of boots that I liked at one time, and I've had my share of cowboy boots as well, but I'm not interested in them anymore, and I've never been a sneaker person unless I am working out. I think men's shoes are somewhat limited in style and design. Herein lay my dilemma. I was not looking for a shoe I could wear daily; I just needed something that would withstand the cold and wet weather upon us right then. Where might I find such a shoe?

I didn't have a plan for how to tackle this daunting task. I was clear about not wanting to spend a lot of money; I was looking for a bargain. I talked about it enough to get an idea about what might work, then I let the idea go and went about my day.

Three days later, I made plans to go downtown looking for fabric to reupholster my sofa with. I continued to put it off—maybe next week, or the week after . . . or maybe next month. A month later, I was planning to head to the fashion district after working out, and I decided to go home first to make breakfast. This would let me avoid the morning traffic headed downtown.

While I was eating breakfast, I thought to myself, "Maybe I can go tomorrow. I'm not really up for the drive." But I got a feeling—I should just do it! I then thought, "Maybe I am meant to go now!"

I gave in to the feeling and went, making my way downtown. It took me a while to find the fabric district in downtown Los Angeles. I decided on a parking structure that charged five dollars a day, instead of paying three dollars for an hour at the meter. I had nothing but time; I could take my time and find the perfect fabric for my sofa. I was walking around with no idea where I was going or what I was doing or what I wanted, but I knew I would know it when I saw it. I love nice fabrics and good fabric stores with trims and pillows and window treatments. Some of the stores had well-designed displays of curtains and color-coordinated fabrics. Store after store was filled with fabric. How does one make a decision? Every time

I walked into a fabulous store, I was surrounded with gracious living. I get this feeling when I see something I love, but I have never had such a feeling for a person. When I am noticing opulence, it fills every fiber of my being with joy and a sense of connectedness to the thing. It can be in a thrift store or a high-end showroom filled with the finest furnishings imaginable; I become one with it, in full appreciation and gratitude for the experience.

I made my way into another fabric store and noticed clear bags of bedding lining the ceiling. I could see that it was full bedding. I asked the price, and the man said it was four hundred and fifty dollars for custom bedding in any fabric of my choice. I thought it was a great deal, and I asked if I could have a closer look; I wanted to see the workmanship. But the guy refused to get one down. "How can I purchase something without examining the merchandise?" I asked. Then I realized that he was not interested in showing me the bedding. I took three more steps towards the back of the store, then realized I shouldn't consider giving this man my business, and walked out.

I went next door and found a silk in a lovely silvery grey with a nice sheen. The ideas started to flow; I had a dark navy and silver fabric, and this would work beautifully with it in my bedroom. I was thinking about everything but the sofa; but then again, I hadn't yet seen the right texture and weight for the sofa. I asked the friendly storekeeper for the price of the fabric and he told me it would be two dollars a yard. I told him I would need twenty yards, I asked for his card, and told him I would call after I measured my window.

Once outside, I decided to just get the fabric and use whatever was left over to make pillows. I'm sure I could find use for any extra fabric. I realized that I needed to transfer money before I made the purchase, and it was taking more time than I had anticipated. I decided to walk around the block, come up the other side, return to the store, and purchase my fabric. I made my way to the corner and turned left. I was having a leisurely walk as I thought about the design of my bedroom and how I could drape the fabric over my bed around the headboard.

Comfortable Shoes

When I reached the opposite corner and was about to make another left, I noticed a shoe store with a nice pair of shoes in the window. I went in for a closer look. A guy I had seen earlier that morning was trying on a nice pair of boots, dark brown with beige stripes on the sides.

The store looked a bit dingy with old carpet and boxes of shoes stacked against the wall on both sides of the room. There was no desk or counter, and it looked as though they were going out of business. I asked the woman if I might try on the shoes on display in a size twelve. She went back to check, and to my surprise, there was no size twelve. I saw an ankle boot with a zipper and asked for the grey and brown in my size, and by the time she returned, I had three more pairs of shoes to ask for. Back to the stock room she went. The boots fit like a glove and they looked nice with my jeans. I asked for the boot the young man was trying on, in both brown and blue. These shoes were reminiscent of the Diesel shoe, with its two-tone solid brown leather with a brighter stripe on both sides. I put them on and loved the fit and the look. "Should a boot fit like a glove?" I asked. "They are a little tight." She assured me that they would stretch.

I inquired about the price, and she said they were thirty dollars. I was a bit surprised. "Why so inexpensive?" She then gave me the sordid details of how the store ended up in disarray. From water damage to employees stealing—I got the full scoop. She did not notice my disinterest; I just wanted some shoes. Nonetheless, she continued like I was a captive audience in a courtroom and she was telling her story under oath. Maybe she thought we were bonding; maybe the excitement of a paying costumer got the better of her and she couldn't stop talking.

I felt good about my choices. I now had two pairs of boots, three pairs of leather shoes—one beige, one string-up, and the third a burgundy loafer. I already owned a couple of pairs of Donald J. Pliner designs, and the last three were similar to those. I kept trying on more shoes, the two leather high-top sneakers and a pair of camel-colored, square-toed mules with straps on the backs. When I finally walked away, I had nine new pairs of shoes and my bill was four hundred and fifty dollars. What a bargain! I could have paid this for one pair of shoes at the mall.

I now had the casual shoes I had needed some weeks earlier. I couldn't have asked for a better price. The shoes were all well made and easy on the eye, and I get compliments on them often—and when I tell the price, most people can't believe it. I continue to give thanks to the universe, which is willing to let me live my wildest dreams.

I am always in the ideal place for the desires of my heart. When I surrender completely, I am reminded of my desires by fully experiencing them as I imagined them and beyond. I am the manifester, holding the desires long enough and then letting go and moving on to the next task, knowing my prayers have been answered. I am always in awe of the universe. It truly does cater to my needs.

Knowing My Worth
I get exactly what I expect

*The moment I decide I am worth more,
so does the universe, and it responds accordingly.*

I was looking for a job and got wind of a men's clothing store hiring an assistant manager. I knew I could do this job with my eyes closed. I set up an interview and said to my roommate, "I need to make at least $2,000 biweekly." At the time, that was a lot of money for me and I knew it would afford me the freedom to be on my own.

I went to the interview and when we came to the part where we discussed money, the manager was hesitant to say what they were willing to offer. I knew I needed to wait and see what his offer would be. He finally said that for this position, they could start me out with two thousand dollars biweekly. I remained calm and collected as I walked out of the store, but internally, I skipped to my car! I had just gotten the money I thought I deserved. I was grateful and excited because I had thought of what I wanted, and I had made it happen! I guess I intended it to happen from a place of expectancy.

The universe does not care about what I am asking for; it only requires me to ask. It is up to me to ask for peace, joy, abundance, love and perfect health. I am redefining myself by what I know, what I deserve. My new perception of self is in my thoughts, words and deeds. What I wish to experience must be at the forefront of my mind on a daily basis. I shall use my words to help change my level of self-worth in every area of my life.

My Second Job
Doing what it takes

*I walk fearlessly forward, trusting
all is in divine order with every step.*

I was working at a gym at the front desk, where I could see a store being built across the street. I had no idea what type of store it was; I only knew that I wanted to get another job, and I had great feelings around the prospect. The store is now finished, a men's clothing store. In fact, it was a would-be designer opening a clothing store to sell a particular clothing line. I dropped my resume and application off and soon afterwards had a great interview. As the interview ended, the manager laughed, "You don't have the job yet!" but I left feeling great, and I did get the job. I can honestly say it was knowingness and a trust that moved me through the process and caused me to feel wonderful about it from start to finish. From the first glance at the space as it was being built to working in the store, I WAS FEARLESS!

A knowing comes over me, a feeling of comfort and ease, with clear instructions about what to do next. It need not make sense to me at the time. The magic comes when I trust and do it anyway. I've taken the time to listen to the truth of my heart and it is enough for me. The universe will give me what I believe is possible, nothing more, nothing less. I must be aware of my feelings about something I say I wish to experience, why it is or is not in my life. This is determined by how I truly feel about a subject.

Delicious Desserts
Completely in the moment

*As I am appreciating, I experience
the truth of who I am.*

I was in a store down the street from my work place when I thought to get some mints. I thought, "What type of mints should I get?" I was looking at the ginger Altoids but decided that it was too big a package; I didn't want so many mints, so I chose something else. A few hours later, a coworker was on his way to the store and asked if I wanted anything. I said, "Yes, some mints." He asked, "What kind?" I responded, "Surprise me." He paused for a second and said, "Okay."

Ten minutes later, he walked in with the mints, and lo and behold, he had bought the ginger Altoids! I could feel the desire for the mints; I could feel the connection to the Altoids. I'd decided to pass on them and I didn't give them a second thought. But that moment of contemplation was enough to bring the mints into my experience. Even as I answered his question, I did not think to ask for the ginger mints.

After work one evening, a lovely coworker and I decided to walk down to the local café for a bite to eat. We were standing at the glass display case drooling over the desserts; I had my eye on a chocolate muffin with dark chocolate chunks. We were like little children, our fingers pressed on the glass, saying, "Ummm, that looks good!" as we pointed to other goodies on display. Then I got into a debate with my friend as to whether I should have such a decadent treat; honestly, the debate was going on in my head and I was voicing this to my friend. This went on for a few minutes, until I decided not to get that scrumptious, dark taste of heaven. We moved on and headed back to work with my vegetarian chili and slices of toast. Yummy!

The next day the gentleman who graciously brought back the ginger mints walked up to me with a brown paper bag. He said he had bought a muffin but could not finish it, and wanted to know if I wanted the other half. I could only eat half, so I said yes. I asked, "what kind is it?" as I reached for the bag. I opened it to find that it was the same scrumptious muffin I had salivated over the day before! This happened in the same week as the mints. I know for sure that it was because I was in the feeling state. In a clear moment of appreciation, everything is possible.

Everything I tune into comes full circle every time I've given it enough energy. I am now choosing my thoughts and words more carefully, knowing the power they possess. The more I notice, the more there is to see. The good and the great—it's up to me what I am choosing to focus on. There is nothing too small for the universe. The universe has the perfect plan for every desire. I must be willing to share my desires.

Working at the Last Minute
Practice what I preach

*I see my world through new eyes,
eyes of love and self-acceptance.*

My feelings tried to warn me. I was asked to help out with a wedding for a friend of a friend, so I agreed to do the flowers. I soon became responsible for doing all the decorations. Every time we would get together, I would say in a sarcastic manner that I don't work at the last minute. I said this on several occasions, and each time, we would all chuckle. I tell you this: when it came time for the wedding, I worked up to the very last minute. I was wrapping the bouquet seconds before the bride walked down the aisle! Although I'd thought I would make a joke to ensure that I would not be working at the last minute, it actually backfired.

I know that I must be clear with my intentions. I must be clear with my desires. I should have said, "All is well, this is fun. I love how everything is flowing, and we have time to spare." I could have praised her for getting the job done in a timely manner. I created the thing I tuned into in my effort to share my desires.

My feelings are always leading me to the best-case scenario. It is up to me to listen, to know myself. In moments of doubt, I am willing to offer a new thought, a new ending. I must see what I wish to happen, and with clarity I offer the best that I can imagine. I will tell a new story—the one I wish to experience. The feeling of truth is always available in every moment. I must have the courage to follow my inner guidance.

All in the Name of Fun
Jokes are creative

*The universe laughs with me, loves with me,
brings me more of me, inspires me
to live a more fulfilling life.*

I needed my own place! I was looking for an apartment in Los Angeles and I had an idea of the location I wanted. There were a few things I had to take into consideration: I wanted to live in a nice clean neighborhood, in a spacious place that had off-street parking. I had seen a number of places, but what is funny about this story is that I got the thing I noticed, the thing I made fun of. In one apartment, I noticed that there was no refrigerator; the young lady said that it would be fifty dollars more if I needed one. I thanked her for her time and as I walked away, I asked myself, "Do you need a refrigerator?" I remember going to work and telling the story of the woman asking if I needed a refrigerator. Do I really need a refrigerator? I don't know. My coworker and I laughed for a few days about this. It was all in fun, and it added a bit of humor to the process of looking for an apartment.

Two weeks later on a Saturday morning, I was up bright and early looking for a place. It was the end of January, the last weekend of the month. I had my list and a clear intention to find a place. All was lined up in my favor. I had a new job, I had the security deposit and great credit. I knew it was time. I knew I had to take the first place I found. I awakened ready to go. I had my list and started making phone calls. The first few numbers

I called went to voice mail. I was a bit dumbfounded—if I were renting an apartment at the end of the month, I would be up with the birds waiting for a call.

This was my train of thought as I hung up the phone. I called another number from my list and a woman answered immediately. She asked me if I wanted to see the place right away, and of course I said yes! I walked in and it seemed nice on the outside. The street was clean, it was a nice building, it was all I desired. I walked up to the building and the front door was open. I let myself in and met the owner, who offered to show me around. The apartment was a bit cluttered; they were re-tiling the bathroom shower and there were wood and work supplies all over the living room. It was a quick tour.

As we walked out to my car, she asked about a credit check; I had my credit report with me. She asked about references, and I told her that I could get them to her. She asked me to call her and give her the information. I called her later that day, but there was no answer; I tried a second time. I began to think that she might not be interested in giving me the place, but said to myself, "Oh, what the heck." I left all of my information, names, and numbers for references, everything she would need to know, on her voice mail. I had surrendered the idea of getting this place.

Just before I made the last phone call to the woman at the apartment building, I had called work to tell them I would be in a little late. I noticed a For Rent sign outside another apartment and decided to call the number; I ended up seeing two more apartments that day, and with the last one, something came over me. I didn't care anymore about meeting a deadline and getting a place before the first of the month. I had surrendered to the fact of having to pay two hundred and fifty dollars for storage and move out five days later. I wanted to avoid having to pay another month for storage. I tell you, in that moment of looking at the last place, it was as if the energy was zapped from me. I couldn't look at another place. It was complete surrender, because the money factor was no longer important. If I had to look for a place next week, it would be okay. I was emotionally tired of looking for an apartment.

I made my way to work and started to settle myself for business. One person wanted to console me by telling me which place she saw me moving into. I am sure she had good intentions; by this time, everyone knew I was in the market for an apartment. One of my coworkers decided to offer an unsolicited reading. I listened without any response; I may have said thank you to be polite, and went on with my day. I believe it was four o'clock when I got a phone call from the lovely woman whom I had met earlier that morning at the first apartment. She said, "It's looking good!" She had a few more calls to make, but she would give me a call back with her final decision. I knew it would work out; I knew it would. Two hours later, I got the phone call: I could move in on Monday or Tuesday. The dilemma of looking for a place was over.

As for the unsolicited reading, it was way off. I now know why the feeling came over me in the last apartment. It is possible that a part of me knew that everything would work out just fine. The beauty of the moment was that I didn't care—I had surrendered in peace. The anxiety was gone when I decided to let go. I didn't care, and I was fine with everything. I was free in the moment of surrender. NO WORRIES!

P.S. I moved in on February second and the landlord met me at my new place with the lease. She was kind enough to fill out the lease agreement while I unpacked the U-Haul. It was in this moment that I realized there was NO REFRIGERATOR! I knew it was because I'd made fun of the statement, "If you need a refrigerator . . ." Talk about the power of words amplified by feelings!

Oh, how I do love to laugh. Energy continues to flow even faster when I am filled with emotions—it doesn't matter which emotions. If I am filled with anger, joy, jealousy or love, it matters not. This is no laughing matter! It is what I want or it is the opposite. I am so inspired by the power that lies within. I must be willing to remember this truth on a daily basis and change my life.

Self-Acceptance
A beautiful reminder

*I am beautiful, and so is my world around me.
It is always reflecting the truth of my thoughts
and feelings in every experience.*

I love dance! I love the clear connection to the divine flow, the spirit that a dancer has. When I watch a group of dancers, my attention is drawn to the person who becomes one with the full experience. Where there is no thinking, just being... it is amazing to watch!

I was out with a friend once, watching professional dancers in a club. It was a mixed crowd, gay, non-gay and undecided, all having a good time. After the full-on dance routine, the dancers were dispersed throughout the club on boxes, and I noticed this one incredible dancer. In that moment, I found myself experiencing truth bumps and feeling at one with this amazing creature. I could only see this individual from the back, and there was no indication as to what the person's gender was. I didn't care—I was mesmerized. This individual had long, beautiful black curly locks cascading past their shoulders. It was a thing of beauty. I moved closer to get a better look and to my surprise, it was a young man. WOW! I was floored! I could see the freedom and confidence flowing through him. I've known all along that your beautiful spirit cannot flow through you if you are worried about what someone thinks. I tell you this: that moment changed my life.

I told all who would listen of my amazing, life-altering experience. When I was back in Florida and flipping through a magazine, I noticed him in a picture with Janet Jackson. I now had a name to go with the face: Nick Florez. I cut the picture out and put it on my refrigerator. A while later, I was watching a music video and noticed a girl dancing, and for the same reason aforementioned, I pointed her out to all my friends who love dance as much as I do. Six months later I was in Los Angeles again and hanging out with my friend, the same guy that had invited me to the club. My time in LA was limited, so I found myself hanging out with him while he was taking care of some errands. This was fine with me; I didn't have any plans, so I thought, "Why not?"

One of the last stops he made was at a dance rehearsal. We were walking up to the dance studio when he noticed a friend and they began to talk. While I stood on the sideline listening, I noticed two guys walking towards us. I immediately recognized one of them, and as they got closer the other was also familiar. It turned out that one of the guys was the guy from the club, the very one on my refrigerator! I was pleased to meet him because of that wonderful experience at the club. I remember telling him how powerful that moment was, and that it is an honor to watch someone be comfortable in their skin. I turned to look in the opposite direction and noticed a girl walking towards us in a hooded sweatshirt. I noticed her bangs. My friend introduced me and began to tell me that she, too, was a dancer—and I recognized her from the video I had been telling my friends to watch. There I was, standing with the two dancers I had been admiring months earlier.

A part of me is re-awakened when I've walked long enough, honoring myself just as I am created. I see my world differently. As I see the beauty from within and from this place, my world begins to change. I see what I am searching for, reflected in a dancer as he allows the energy to flow through him, becoming one with the music—allowing the music to move his body. He is divine grace for being in the moment, without hesitation, expressing himself freely, beautifully, completely. This part of him is a part of me that longs to be expressed fearlessly.

The Perfect Table
It's just an idea

*Words and affirmations shall be my
healing power and magic wand.*

I was excited to move into my new apartment. I had furniture I had purchased in Florida. I had no idea what type of place I would have, but I knew I would be moving to Los Angeles. To get into the fullness of the experience of moving back to LA, I decided to shop for furniture. This process started six months to a year before I actually moved. I had a U-Haul filled with furniture. Now that I'm thinking about it, I realize how backwards it feels now writing about it. It feels in this moment as if I should have bought furniture once I got to my destination. I remember now that I wanted to bring my car and I didn't want to put the miles on it. To rent a U-Haul would be the wiser thing to do.

When I arrived in my new space in LA, I discovered that the table I'd purchased in Florida was too big for the dining space. I got it at a thrift store and paid less than fifty dollars for it. I had to face the truth: I needed to find a new table. I began to think of the ideal table. I thought a round table would be the way to go. I set out to find my table. I knew I didn't want to spend more than one hundred dollars, and I knew it was possible, because I had looked around at a number of second-hand stores. I did not intend to look for a solid wood table at full retail price, and besides, I love finding the right piece at the right price. So off to the thrift stores I went. I was hopeful, excited and willing to look any- and everywhere I felt guided to look. I was feeling great, in a place of expectancy, with a knowingness—I knew I would find it. It was just a matter of time. Some time passed but I was still filled with the idea of having a round table. I had seen a couple of tables on my journey but none was the right one.

When I first arrived in California, I lived in Culver City. I would walk to a little restaurant a few blocks from my home to get out of the house, get some fresh air and a bite to eat. I would sit and enjoy my meal in a state of gratitude. During one of my restaurant trips, I noticed a thrift store across the street. I thought, "Wouldn't it be nice to pay them a visit, just to have a look?" But I headed home instead.

A year later, on my way to work, I had my own place and was now in search of a round, wooden dining table. I was a little early so I decided to stop at the little restaurant in Culver City for a bite to eat. It was just like old times. I was feeling great! I was sitting in my old seat facing the window, looking out at the thrift store across the street, when something caught my eye. I finished my lunch and headed over there. I was walking around and noticed a round wood table with a price tag for $100—my heart began to race. I had found my table! I wondered how I would get it home, and found out that the store delivered. It all worked out in perfect order.

I am clear in the method of manifesting. It is a knowing that brings forth ease and grace. In this place, there are no worries. I fill myself with the desire by doing the action in joy, and the rest is in the flow of perfection with this well-balanced act.

I excitedly held the intention, knowing my table would present itself for the price I desired. Flowing gracefully into my experience, looking every now and again for my table, but not really searching, I was giving just enough attention to manifest what I wanted. I did appreciate the table, but decided to give it to a friend. I was now without a dining room table again. I wanted to get something a little bigger. I tell you I found another table just like the one I had given away. I paid ninety-five dollars for it and it's the perfect size. Everything happened within six weeks.

Hardwood Floors and a Fireplace
My words are made manifest

*I use my words wisely calling forth
what I love and what I wish to experience.*

I was living in Los Angeles, California and looking for my own place. I knew the power of words. I wondered how I could answer the question "Have you found a place?" I thought I would answer, "No! But when I do find a place, it will have hardwood floors and a fireplace." Most people would laugh, but I knew it would work. I was clear: I knew I wanted a one-bedroom with a place where I could meditate. I did find a place, and it did have hardwood floors and a small room where I could meditate. Two out of three was not bad, but I ended up moving back to Florida—and I promise you, the first place I rented there had hardwood floors and a fireplace with a small room off the master bedroom in which I could meditate. The house after that had hardwood floors and a fireplace. I believe you get the picture. The place I am living in as I am writing this has hardwood floors and a fireplace. Ten years later, I am still manifesting hardwood floors and a fireplace!

I know the power of my words and I use them intentionally to manifest my desires. I only need to continue to appreciate hardwood floors to find them in my experience. I know the things I give my attention to will soon become a part of my life. I know the universe will continue to bring forth all I am focused on.

My Mental Shopping List
Ask and you shall receive

I am manifesting with grace in miraculous ways.

I had moved into my new place and thought of some things I needed. After the packing was finished, I didn't think to make a list. It was in the back of my mind that there were a few more things I could use. It's apparent that it was not my top priority, because it had been almost a year and I had not purchased the items from my mental list. I had gone shopping on several occasions and bought anything and everything but the things on my list.

I had a client that stopped by my work place on a Sunday evening to tell me she was moving back to New York and had some things she wanted to get rid of. The following morning I was taking a shower, using a soap that smelled lovely. I was getting into the appreciation place of fully experiencing the fragrance, the way it lathers, the smooth way it slid down my arm. I was caressing my arm with this heavenly smell and I wondered where I had purchased the soap. I had to have more! I went so far as to think how my lover would like that sweet-smelling scent.

I got dressed and was on my way to my client's house. It looked as though she was having a yard sale, and there were all sorts of things on the front lawn. She was moving away and could not take half of the things in the storage pod and on the lawn because she was shipping everything.

My Mental Shopping List

I was looking through some boxes and noticed a toaster, which was something on my mental list. I had wanted a teapot, as well, not just any teapot, but a glass teapot with the flowering tea. I had been at a garage sale a couple of weeks before and noticed a cute little iron teapot, but I didn't have any teacups, so I opted not to get it. I now have two teapots, one iron pot, and the other glass. Just what I wanted. I told my client how I had been thinking of these things, and then she offered me a full knife set. It was a nice set of knives in every size! This too was on my list. Now I found myself with everything on my mental list, everything!

As I was helping my friend, I saw two small boxes sitting on the ground and I asked her what was in them. She said, "Soap, you want one?" I went to have a look before responding, and as I opened the box, there before my eyes was the very soap I had showered with less than two hours earlier. I couldn't believe it— the very soap I had been appreciating, and I now had a box of four, and the location from where to purchase them.

I played a part in my client's manifested need to clear out her pod by the following morning, which we made happen, and I helped as much as I could to help her meet her deadline. Thank you again for playing a part in manifesting my desire.

While out shopping, I had bypassed most of these items on more than two occasions. I had not given them a second thought. I could not have planned for such an experience. I now realize my disinterest in the things from my list. The universe had other plans—it makes sense now. Everything I wanted was out on the lawn, down to my new favorite soap.

The Perfect Vacation
The past can't touch me

*I have a clear vision of my desires, and
the universe gives me validation daily for right action.*

I was planning a trip to visit my family in Florida. It was routine that I stay with an ex-roommate and sleep on the couch. I could not do it this time though, and I didn't want to stay with my family. I do love them, but it's wonderful when you can leave. I must also add that we don't have a lot in common. There are only so many times you can talk about the good old days. I knew my friend's house would not be much different.

I moved forward with my plans to go to Florida; I called my friend Karen Crabtree to tell her of my arrival date. Karen replied, "I was going to call you to ask if you wanted to stay at my house!" She then said, "I had no idea why you were calling, but I thought, Why don't I ask him if he wants to stay with me?" I told her my arrival date, and she said, "I am leaving that day to fly to Italy. I will be gone for ten days, but you can have use of the car and the house while I am away." Great! Thank you!

I was not sure how long I would be visiting, but I told her I would see her when she returned, and I'd pick her up from the airport. Talk about perfect timing. I found that I would be in town longer than I'd expected.

The Perfect Vacation

Before I'd moved away, a friend had extended an invitation, asking me not to hesitate to call when I came back to visit. I did just that. It was the Wilsons, Kent and Phillipa and their three beautiful children. It was a wonderful experience. They were very generous and accommodating. My experience in Florida turned out to be more than I could have imagined. I had the feeling of not going back to a certain vibrational environment. The feelings were pretty strong. I did go visit my family on a regular basis.

Life meets me at every turn to assist me on my journey. I have unconditional support in what I believe is possible. This allows me to evolve at my own pace. When it is time to move on, I am in agreement with the best life has to offer. And so it is. By healing myself first, I am the example.

My Dream Job
I am my first student

My life is a reflection of what I love.

Some years ago, I was listening to Wayne Dyer's "Manifest Your Destiny" tape, the morning and evening meditations. I found I was more inclined to meditate in the mornings. I began to do the meditation on a semi-regular basis. I wanted to create a routine I could follow. I always sat in the same chair in the corner of the room, from which I had a full view of the living room. I had the curtains open; I could see the overgrown, lush green plants dancing with the wind outside my window, which was calming. I was looking forward to letting go, and I came to enjoy the feelings. I looked forward to the sense of peace.

While in this peaceful place, I would imagine that whatever I was meant to do must come from within me. It had to be something I possessed now! It wasn't about going to school or working at another job that didn't inspire me. In those moments, it was about trust. I let go and for about three months, I met myself on a semi-regular basis.

At the time, I was working in a hair salon. I remember a friend asking me, "Why would you work in an environment where you have to shut down, when your life is about opening up?" What a powerful question! At the time, I had no answer. It has been challenging at times, but I did what I had to do—suck it up and keep going. I knew it wasn't my lifelong punishment. I repeated this realization over and over in my mind like a mantra, which made it a bit more tolerable. I knew I would be moving on.

While meditating, I was in a more free-flowing space. I was tuned into the feeling of my desire. I wasn't concerned with an idea, but with the feeling of what I could or would be doing. The more I meditated, the better I began to feel. It was a place without concern. I wasn't thinking about anything. I didn't want to think thoughts that could pull me from this place. The 'hows' would get my mind into trying to figure it out. Somewhere inside me, I felt safe and carefree. I knew that regardless of what happened, I would be okay. I had this feeling that I was without needing anything from anyone. I say this because I didn't need anything to access this space—it was my desire to meet with myself, Just me, no need for distractions. I wanted to change my life.

I was feeling more secure, knowing that my life would be changing. I had made plans to visit Los Angeles. I had also planned to give my two weeks' notice to the salon. I returned to Florida without any real prospects for a new job and worked for one week without mentioning my plans to give my two-week notice. On the last day of that week, one of the owners asked if she could speak with me. We walked outside, and it turned out that she was letting me go. I listened with an inner smile, knowing things were moving forward.

My friend finished, giving me a wonderful explanation as to why they were going to have to let me go. She was crying, but I was smiling at the universe for pushing things along. I guess it was hard for her, but she had no idea that I had been planning to quit, and I didn't feel the need to mention it at that point. I assured her that I would be fine and said my goodbyes.

I was now at a loss, because I had responsibilities that needed my attention. I needed work! I had gotten a lead that my old job was looking for an assistant manager, and I was willing to do something to meet my obligations. I think there was only one familiar face when I went for my interview. I met with the general manager and had a great interview, during which I shared my concerns about the past and my thoughts about what I could bring to the new team. The store had gone through major changes, from downsizing to undergoing an internal makeover. The bottom line, I got the gig.

I started the following week. My first day was somewhat interesting, but after that, I was bored beyond bored. There is nothing worse than six people trying to look busy refolding clothes for five hours! I knew that I'd made the wrong move, but I tried to talk myself into staying. By midday, I knew I could not do it. You may wonder how hard it could be to motivate a small team, keeping them busy and ensuring they meet their goals for the day, but by this time, it was crystal clear. I remember talking to the one familiar face, telling him I was leaving. There was a feeling in me that would not let me move forward. If I am truthful, the feeling started the first night on my way home from the store. The drive there was even more powerful than the night before. I knew there was no way I could do it. The feelings were too strong. I felt like a fish out of water.

When I told my friend of my desire, her response was, "You can at least work one full week." I told her there was no way I could, even if I wanted to. The following day was Wednesday, the district manager was coming in, and it was my turn to take her outside for a talk. I expressed my feelings and thanked her for giving me the opportunity. She was very nice and gave me the option to leave then or at two o'clock, when the other manager was getting in. I thought about staying, but it was a moment of freedom. I couldn't wait—I had to leave. The district manager was very understanding. I had no idea where I was going, but I didn't have that negative feeling anymore. I knew I had done the right thing.

I am sure every one of us can remember a time when we had a very strong feeling that told us one thing or another. We all have that inner guidance. This time I was listening, and my feelings made sure of it. It is amazing to look back and see my wish being fulfilled with the full participation of the universe. I can see from my clear intention, which conjured the feelings and words that would lead the way.

I've listened to my feelings when I've been without work and had car payment, rent to pay, and everything else that goes along with being a responsible adult. The time came when I could no longer afford my place and had to move in with a friend. I got a call from a friend who wanted me to decorate his new home. Once again, I was doing something I knew how to do. It was something flowing out of me—I had always decorated my own place to the nines. I had taken classes here and there that would give me the insight I needed to create the ideal space. If that didn't work, I could have my client choose a look and duplicate it. The best design comes from a place of freedom of expression.

I used to do floral arrangements by memory; it worked out well, and I saved my clients thousands of dollars. I did this for years and not once did I make business cards or a portfolio; everything was word-of-mouth. I am still amazed by the flow. To this day, I am in the flow. I am more fulfilled than ever before teaching what I believe—love and live. I am my first student.

I am moving through life doing what I love, being of service. I continue to move forward one breath at a time as I am reminded of truth by my brother's eyes. I awaken with the choice to make a difference in the world.

The Round Ottoman
The perfect accessory

On a daily basis, I look for something to appreciate.

I am flowing in abundance, fully aware that we are all the same.

Sometime ago, I spent most of the morning catching up with my friend Renee. She mentioned taking a tour of the 'Street of Dreams' last week, it's an opportunity to see million dollar homes, and I was looking forward to it. My friend Karen Crabtree had gone the year before, and I knew that I was definitely interested in doing it myself. It sounded like heaven. I can spend hours, maybe days, in a good furniture store filled with fabulous designs and styles, a decorator's fantasy come true. I look at the full room: the walls, the intent of the designer and the person in charge of the visuals for that particular store. I truly get swept away by the beauty; it's a feeling that comes over me. This has been the case for as long as I can remember. I am put into a trance induce state by opulence.

The thought of going into a multimillion-dollar home specifically created to inspire potential clients in every area—what better way could I spend my day? I'm sure the tour attracted builders, designers, architects, and potential homeowners. This was a chance I was not going to pass up. I asked Renee if she would be interested in going again, and to my surprise she agreed. We jumped into the car to rush there, since we did not know what time the tour would end. We entered this huge parking lot that reminded me of a theme park's parking lot. I was excited because Renee had a magazine from her previous tour, and from what I could see, it would be well worth the trip.

We found a parking space and made our way to the shuttle. I know... just like at a theme park. In keeping with the theme park theme, there was a cover charge. There were people everywhere, at least two hundred people, families, babies in strollers couples, and children. There were people trampling across the impeccable landscapes, trying not to be noticed. The only things missing were a Ferris wheel, cotton candy and the stench of corn dogs.

People were walking from mini-mansion to mini-mansion. There was something for everyone. I walked in a daze, touring and taking in all the details. I was being inspired from the inside out! It was a feeling of complete bliss. I walked from one place to the next, trying to remember the ideas I wanted to use for my own projects, and just when I thought it couldn't get any better, when I thought nothing could top this, the next place would leave me breathless. One house overwhelmed me with its color scheme and outdoor bathtub—this was truly brilliant. I've seen showers and hot tubs, but never had I seen a full antique tub with claw feet set behind a glass wall that separated the waterfall shower from the outside tub. It was romantic, hot and sexy. In the master suite, there was more fabulousness; a beautiful round ottoman was one of the focal points of the room. I made a comment to my friend, "I must get a round ottoman." This one was a tufted soft powder-grey, with inverted pleats and piping—exquisite! I made up my mind that this would be my next mission.

A couple of weeks later, I got a call for a consultation with a would-be client about some ideas for her newly purchased home. Upon entering the home, I could see that it was quite nice and she and her husband didn't need my help. They were doing just fine without me. The house had a great layout with an open floor plan. From the front door, I could see a full view of the living room, dining room and kitchen. Off the kitchen was a small dining area with a tall square bar table. The colors were sage and light beige, a nice blend that complimented the chocolate brown leather furniture. I walked though the house giving my opinion. When we got to the bedroom, it was tropical and had a matching bed, dressers, armoire, and end tables. There was too much furniture in this small bedroom, and at the foot of the bed there was a round thing covered with a floral slipcover.

I asked, "What's this?" My client said that it was an ottoman and they didn't have a place for. I suggested they move it to the living room. Once we moved the ottoman, we were in agreement; it did look better in the living room. I met with her the next day, and it turned out that her husband didn't like it there. He wanted to use the piece he purchased, which was fine with me. I am never forceful; after all, I don't have to live there. The wife did like the idea of having the ottoman there, but now they had the ottoman and no space for it. I thought to myself, "Is this the way I'm going to get my round ottoman?" I told her that if she were interested in selling it, I would be more than happy to take it off her hands.

It would be a few weeks before I returned, and when I did, my client mentioned that someone had asked her about the ottoman, and now she thought she might keep it. It was now a hot commodity, so I asked her where she found it. She gave me the name and location of a used furniture store, but added that it had been more than six months since she'd bought it. I went to the store for weeks and nothing showed up. I had seen round ottomans around, but none close to the image I had in mind. I had met a designer who knew a furniture maker, and I asked her whether he could make a round ottoman. She didn't know, but said she would get back to me. I continued working on other clients' homes while keeping my eyes open for my ottoman.

I had found a picture of the exact one I wanted and put it into my dream book. One Saturday morning I was speaking to my designer friend and she told me that the furniture maker could, in fact, make the ottoman, but it would take a while. I said to her, "I am not going to believe that I can't find a round ottoman. I am not going to believe it!"

I was supposed to meet with a client later that day, but he was running a little late. I decided to go back to the very first location. I guess it was in my being, the desire for the ottoman was in me, but on that day, it wasn't at the forefront of my mind. I walked into the store, walked the floor from front to back, and found no ottoman. On the way out, I looked down in the same direction as when I'd entered, and there before me was my round ottoman! I found it! I found it! I didn't see it when I was walking the same path, but it was there on my way back. Imagine that!

This one was plaid, dark burgundy with pale gold stripes, and it had the piping and inverted pleats. I would have it reupholstered to my taste and it was only eighty dollars. I couldn't wait to get it home. I put it in the trunk of my car and was off. I had manifested my ottoman. I knew it would eventually show up, this I knew for sure.

In case you are wondering, it took forty-four days from when I put the image in my dream book to when I found my ottoman.

I tuned in to the beauty and knew it would be mine. Without doubt, I moved forward awaiting direction from the universe. At first glance, I knew it was the thing I would manifest next. I had a clear image of what I wanted. I had come across a few ottomans, but the perfect one would find its way into my home. It is a knowing that I cannot ignore, trusting that I will have what I desire.

There is No Such Thing as an Accident
There are no accidents, I should know
I am consciously aware of what I am manifesting.

Life is beautiful; it's a wonderful day. My thoughts were flowing all over the place. I'd just had a dream that a friend repaid the thousand dollars he had borrowed from me; I had resigned myself to the fact that it was a gift. I was happy to be free of that relationship; we had grown apart, and longevity does not necessarily make for a harmonious relationship. I was free, and if it was the thousand dollars that made it uncomfortable for him to call and say hello, I considered it money well spent.

I was pulling out of my parking space in the underground structure when I noticed how close I had parked to the wall. I thought, "You should be more careful when parking. You don't want to scratch your car." My next thought was, "I will be even more careful when I get my new car."

I was in a place of bliss, loving the wonderful dream. I was contemplating life and all its wonder.

I made a left turn onto Wilshire Blvd. and headed home feeling amazing. I had a wonderful workout, did some shopping, life was great! What a way to start the day. Even though I work out five days a week, I continue to give thanks each day.

There Is No Such Thing As An Accident

I was brought back to reality by the sound of screeching tires. I looked to my right and a car was headed straight for me—there was no time to react! I didn't have time to brace myself, it was happening.

Crash, the car hit my car.

It was quick and painless. I felt the jolt of my body as the car ran into the passenger-side front door; my car was pushed into the far left lane.

It was morning, between 8:30 and 9:00 a.m.—talk about perfect timing, there were no cars in either lane.

After the crash, I pulled over to the far right side of the road. I went to make sure the driver of the other car was not injured. She was a little shaken but had no bodily injuries.

We exchanged insurance information. It turned out that it happened across the street from her work place and within a mile of my home. Another woman ran to the scene; I am assuming she was the manager from her work place. She insisted that we exchange information; she wasn't interested in calling the police.

I went home, called my insurance company and hers to report the accident, and after that, there wasn't any more I could do. After the long phone calls, I had time to think about what had happened.

My first thoughts were, "How could I have gotten into an accident? I am a great driver." I take that street every day. I was a bit puzzled, to say the least. I believe in the law of attraction. I was aware of my feelings before the accident, and I tell you, I was feeling amazing! For a moment, I was a little skeptical about good vibrations and "like attracting like."

I like to think I'm a pretty positive person; I'm aware of my feelings on a regular basis. On the morning of this beautifully orchestrated encounter, I was in heaven. I watched in astonishment as it unfolded before my eyes.

I was trying to understand how I could find myself in such an experience. Just seconds before the car hit, I was in a very happy place emotionally. The idea that my entire belief system was invalid gave me a moment of fear. What if everything I had been experiencing until that moment made no sense? The practice of being in good spirits, tuning to a positive vibration, etc., would have no validity.

It was a bit overwhelming. I didn't know what to trust! I thought, Where are my angels? Why didn't they warn me of this crash? I had relied on my feelings for so many years for guidance. I now found myself in an experience that was not in alignment with my feelings... or so I thought!

It would be nice to take some time off from work and go visit my family back in Florida. This had been my train of thought some weeks before the crash. I had been working seven days a week for the last eight months, from open to close, ten- to twelve-hour shifts. This went on without one day off.

The catch for me was that I truly love what I do.

It worked out perfectly. It was all part of the master plan.

I was now ready to take some time off from work. I missed my mother and wished to go for a visit. I thought I would take two weeks off to go see her, maybe at the end of July. I also thought I could put my car in the shop while I was on vacation... all was well.

I am not interested in watching television, it's one of the reasons I don't have cable. I am clear in the fact that all I am tuned into is offering an energy, a vibration. I know the effects of being engaged in inharmonious conversations, books, and television.

I'd like to shed light on the questions I asked earlier. How did I find myself in such an experience? Knowing what I know, it took some time to retrace my thinking, and I eventually came to this delightful conclusion.

On a daily basis, I use the internet. I usually ignore or tune out the news headlines and go about my business, but this day was different. I noticed a headline about a plane crash and one thirteen-year-old survivor. I remember getting interested in the story, reading every detail. The story consumed me. I needed to know more. As I read further, I felt an emotional connection with the girl and her relatives. I had a visual image of her in the hospital bed and the doctors not telling her that her mother had died in the plane crash. I was all about the plane crash!

I went to work, but I didn't ask anyone if they had heard about the plane crash. While I was at work, a person came in for a session and said they were happy to find another reader, because their old reader had died. I had been reading about a plane crash, and now this. Later that day, I was doing a reading for another client and mentioned a name to her; she paused for a moment and said that the only person she knew with that name had died in a plane crash. What? I sat in silence as fear of the unknown tried to take me over. I started to follow the trail of fear, but I continued with the reading.

I didn't say, "Oh what a coincidence! I'm taking a plane flight to visit my family in Florida." Shortly afterward, I tuned into another story on the internet about a plane crash. By this point, I had developed a full-blown fear of flying. I remember asking out loud, "Are you guys trying to tell me something?" I was speaking to God, the angels, my guides, anyone who was listening.

It was clear that I needed to shift my energy. I began reading a book by Stuart Wilde, thinking it would take my mind off my new fear. I wasn't going to back down unless there was some indisputable sign to keep me from getting on that plane. I was going to see my mother, and nothing was going to stop me! Not even the possibility of a plane crash.

In his book Silent Power, Wilde mentioned taking a leisurely flight. I thought that sounded wonderful! I could do that; I have taken more than my share of leisurely flights. I started to feel better.

I was excited to go visit my family, and I was talking with one of the girls at work about it. I said to her, "I know what I will do on the day of my flight. I will busy myself all day, and when it's time to leave I will be exhausted." She interrupted me, adding, "Then you could crash!" I knew what she meant, but it didn't stop a wave of energy from flowing over my entire body, filling every fiber of my being with uncertainty. I didn't respond. I thought for a moment and said, "Yes, I could sleep the entire way home."

It all came full circle. The following day on my way home from the gym, I stopped by the store and to my surprise, I manifested the crash. I did not know it at the moment of impact, but I did think, "Here is the crash!"

I speak from a place of truth when I say that there are no such things as accidents. I found myself in an experience that would prove me right. After the initial shock, I could trace my thoughts to the event at the start of the week, before it had manifested into my experience. The thought of my potential as a manifester is overwhelming—I can't stop myself from manifesting! It is who I am, who all of us are. I know from first-hand experience the importance of all I give my attention to: what I am plugged into for the sake of catching up, joking around, and in the name of entertainment, and the impact it all has on my life.

The Lakers Fan
Fond memories

*It is my intention to experience
the joys of life on a daily basis.*

In 1984, I became a Los Angeles Lakers fan. I have played basketball since I was ten years old, and I had watched some Lakers games on TV, but it was not until my dad and I went to the Forum and sat ten rows back from the floor that the excitement of the crowd, enthusiasm of the teams, and the lights and music got me hooked.

Flash forward to my manifestation list of 2004. I would go to games once every few years, but mostly I watched them on television. I love anything live. Sporting events, concerts, anything; so I wrote on my list, "I am attending more live events this year. Concerts, plays, sporting events, and especially Lakers games."

By the end of 2004, I had attended eight home games and several concerts. I had two friends with season tickets that called me up either to invite me or to offer me tickets they were unable to use. This has continued to this day. In the 2009-10 season, I attended almost every home game. My neighbors designed the opening show for the Lakers and I started assisting them at the games. I have been privileged to help them and to have been on the floor at the start of those games... what a dream come true! It was on the list. Something I felt silly putting on there, but it is something I like to do. I am so happy that I was able to laugh at myself a little and then to graciously accept the ways that this is manifesting in my world.

I love life and spending time with my family. The joy of sharing is something we both love. It is the gift that keeps on giving. I will always cherish these memories. I am eternally grateful for those times.

The Manifested Jacket
Wouldn't it be nice?

My ideas flow freely with ease daily.

I created a vision board with cutouts of everything I liked from the Patagonia clothing catalog. I put the word Free on it, hung it in my room, and looked at it often with excitement. My goal was to become a musical ambassador for companies like this. I was very excited, knowing that it would show up. One day my friend called me while driving by the Patagonia store and said he was guided to tell me to go in there before they closed that day. I struck up a conversation with a woman there and while we were talking, I noticed a contest for a free clothing item: I could pick any item in the store and put my name in the drawing to win. I did it without thinking, excited about the opportunity, and picked a jacket that I really needed. It was very cold in my house in December, and the clothes I had were not warm enough. They called me two days later and said I had won! When I was in the store a week before the contest, I'd told an employee that my goal was to be an ambassador, when I stopped by to pick up my jacket, he said, "I can't believe you won!"

I put the image on my vision board and the word Free and left the details to the universe. It was a surprise to get the call that I won. The power of focus is amazing. It is what I really needed and it came at the perfect time. I am always grateful for the support of the universe.

Seeing Beyond the Illusion
Blind Faith

I am in a constant state of love and self-acceptance.

One day last December, my roommate moved out suddenly and without notice. I needed to cover his portion of the rent. Standing in front of the kitchen sink, washing scraps of food off the dishes, I was minding my own business and thinking about how I was going to come up with the missing rent money. I kept thinking of all I was grateful for and maintaining the disciplines that my spiritual adviser and all his recommended readings had outlined: "Be in the feeling space of what you want... act as if you already have what you desire... get clear, feel good and get excited." I have to admit, it does requires work and discipline to pretend that all is well when you have a three-day eviction notice on your plate.

No pun intended. My adviser's words pierced my mind and I was determined to do everything in my power to fix my situation. As I rinsed my last fork, I had a few rational ideas, followed by an irrational one. They went something like this: "I'll sell my camera for $500... I'm going to post it on craigslist.com today. YES! That's what I'll do. I refuse to worry. Okay, stay positive... I will do that... hopefully someone will respond today! Wait

… not 'hopefully,' I WILL have it today… hmm, yes… (is that my phone I hear?)… what I really, really desire is for someone to just GIVE ME $500! Oh, wouldn't that be great!" I giggled and thought, "Now that's thinking big." Despite the stress of my situation, I played my adviser's encouraging words in my mind over and over, I stayed hopeful even though at times my rational mind would laugh at me and think I was crazy for feeling happy and cheerful during this crisis. SHHHH!

I quickly replaced the doubtful thoughts with positive thoughts of my son, my most prized blessing. As I reached for the dish-towel, I noticed my phone and realized I'd missed a call. I dialed the number and found that it was a good friend of mine who had called to get my address because he was sending Christmas cards. He said he had a gift for me and asked how I was doing. I was hesitant to tell him, especially because I was still in such a good feeling space and didn't want to drag the conversation down with my worries, but I told him anyway. To my surprise, a joyful blessing manifested right before my very existence.

He told me he was playing Santa this year because he'd been doing very well with his consulting business and wanted to spread the wealth by sending a few people a gift of $500. What? Really? Wow! I immediately knew that God, my angels and the universe were working through my friend to provide their heavenly assistance. With each one of his words, I felt their comfort, love and support. Tears of relief and joy wet my smiling cheeks. This miracle confirmed everything that my spiritual adviser had been saying from the very beginning: "Trust, believe, manifest!"

I immediately called my adviser to share my story. Now I live expecting good things always. I'm so excited! THANK YOU!

I am willing to move through life, choosing thoughts and words that bring me closer to my desires. I am willing to use my words to shift my energy. I know it will take complete surrender and focus. I am more aware of my words and desires being in alignment with what I wish to experience.

A Perfect Smile
Finding a dentist

*I ask and surrender, knowing all is taken care of.
I trust my feelings and listen for guidance from within.*

I was thinking of finding a dentist. I was new to the area and had gotten a number some time ago for a dentist, but I'd never followed through. Six months later, I really needed to find a dentist. I had spoken with a potential client who wanted to come by before leaving for a trip. A good friend had referred her and I wanted to make it happen. I was pretty busy, but told her she could come by for a reading on her way to the airport. She came by around 8:30 that night.

I answered the door to find a sweet young lady who reached out for a hug as she asked to use the bathroom. The session lasted for an hour and she was off. Before leaving, she said, "I'm a dentist, and the wonderful thing is, I am the only working dentist in the building. We can do trade!"

Who says someone won't come knocking at your door? I was not sitting around waiting, but I had clarified my intention months earlier about needing a dentist. I was reminded a few days before a dentist showed up. I'd just had a passing thought about getting to the dentist.

A Visit to California
Manifesting the money I need

*When I trust my feelings I feel at ease,
and I know I am moving in the right direction.*

My mother was complaining to me one morning before she was about to go on a trip across country to visit my brother and watch his children while he and his wife went away for a few days. She would be gone for a week, yet she had absolutely no spending money to take with her. I asked her how much she thought she needed.

"Well," she said, "it would be nice to have $500, but I haven't had any work in a while, so I only have about $40.00 in my wallet…"

So I said to her, "okay, well, if you want $500.00, then claim it to the universe. Say out loud that you need $500.00."

"No, that's silly," she said. "Who would hear me?"

"The universe will hear you," I replied, "And the universe will conspire to bring it to you if you have faith and conviction in your heart. Do you believe that you need $500.00?"

"Yes," she said.

"Do you believe you deserve $500.00?" I asked.

"Yes," she answered.

"Okay then, say it out loud. Shout it out!" I urged her to shout it out as loud as she could, many times, until it came out of her throat more and more naturally and with greater conviction. After she was done shouting, I said quietly, "And so it is." We both felt a great sense of peace come over us. My mother headed for the airport and I continued on my way to work.

The next morning I had a voice mail on my phone. It was my mother.

"You will never believe what happened!" she said excitedly. "I got to your brother's house and he sat down with me at his kitchen table to describe the children's routine before he and his wife went away. After he was done listing everything out, he handed me an envelope. "What is this?' I asked. "It's a little money in case you need to buy anything while we are away." You will never guess how much was in that envelope! She was virtually screaming into my answering machine. I already knew the answer. "Exactly 500.00!"

Having the courage to trust landed me the five hundred dollars I had asked for. I knew in my heart that everything would work out, and it did. It is exactly what I asked for and more. It is about looking beyond the illusion and seeing what I want. This day I had a clear vision of the five hundred dollar... the universe handled the details.

A Big Favor
I trust that all is well

I listen for guidance from within.

My sister needed a loan. I knew it was important because she had never asked to borrow money before. She did not specify an amount and said she would take whatever I could share. At the time, I was a freelance worker and wasn't sure where my next check was coming from. I thought to send her two hundred and fifty dollars. This was a thought, and behind this thought was a feeling and a thought simultaneously. I felt that I should send five hundred dollars. For a moment, I thought, No! I will send two fifty. The feeling came over me to send the five hundred. There was a feeling of peace and excitement at the thought of surprising my sister with five hundred. I was fearless when sending it, knowing all would work out. It was Friday when the money was sent through Western Union, and I tell you, on Monday I had five hundred dollars in unexpected cash. I had trusted my feeling that everything was fine, and it was.

When you are in a place of peace and calm, you can hear the guidance from within. The more you are interested in getting to know yourself, truly listening to your inner voice, the better your life will be. It is from this place that the best you have to offer must reside. More importantly, from this place all the answers are available to you. Something as simple as who might I call for assistance.

We Need a Vacation
Our Miami trip

My desires are clear I see only the end result.

My partner and I would like to share one of our many manifesting stories with you. We own a trucking company. On January 1, 2010, the port of Long Beach and Los Angeles was closed to trucks built before 2008. Since our company only owned trucks older than 2007, we knew that come January first, we would be out of business. On December 8, 2009, Marlene and I decided to take our family on a three-week vacation to Miami, leaving on June 16, 2010. When we booked the flights, we were certain that we would be unemployed at that point and ready to take a long trip of relaxation.

All that changed on January 19, 2010, just over one month after making those reservations. We began a new venture and opened up our spiritual shop on Sunset Blvd. in Los Angeles, called the House of Intuition. After opening up the shop, our desire to go to Miami shifted. Marlene and I both kept saying that we wished we hadn't bought those tickets and that it would be great if we could get our money back. The timing for the trip was not good and we really needed to stay in Los Angeles for HOI. As our trip got closer and closer, my anxiety grew worse.

During the months leading to June 16, we were attending regular workshops at our shop that taught the power of manifesting. During class, the speaker would tell us that all we have to do is ask, and the universe will

We Need A Vacation

respond to our vibration.

Exactly one week before the flight, I began putting all my energy and thoughts into not making this trip happen. I began by praying and asking the Spirit to take care of this trip and lit candles every day asking for my prayers to be heard. I even looked at the possibilities of changing my flights and coming home earlier, but that option was way too expensive. I started telling everyone and myself how I wanted to stay in California and not go to Miami. I was thinking about how great it would feel to be able to stay and enjoy my new shop without having the guilt and worry of leaving it for three weeks.

The call came in just six days before I was due to fly. On June 11, my brother phoned me from Miami and said that the pilots of Spirit Airline might go on strike. I could not believe it. This was the airline that I was to fly on in just six days! After hanging up the phone with my brother, I went online—sure enough, there it was. The pilots of Spirit Airline were threatening to strike at midnight if the airline didn't reach an agreement about their pay increase and benefits. I read further and learned that the last airline strike had been in 2001; this negotiation between the pilots and Spirit Airline had been going on for three years. There I was, anxious until midnight for the announcement of a resolution or a decision to strike. Every hour the negotiation was extended to the following hour, and finally, after three a.m., I could no longer stay up. Before I lay my head on my pillow, I said one last prayer to the universe to make this happen: "I do not want to go to Miami. Please make it possible for me to stay." I woke up at eight a.m., and right away I got online: there it was! The pilots of Spirit Airlines had walked off the job. All flights for Saturday, June 12 and Sunday, June 13 had been canceled. On Sunday the airline announced that flights for the next two days had been canceled. I was now a nervous wreck, checking all day long until Monday afternoon at five p.m., when the airline sent out a press release announcing that they had canceled all flights for Wednesday, June 16, because they could not come to an agreement with their pilots. I began running around my house like a five-year-old child at Disneyland. I was screaming, "They canceled our flights! We are getting all our money back, and we get to stay! I manifested that! I manifested that!"

On Tuesday, June 16, the airline put out one more press release, announcing that they had come to an agreement and their planes would be back in the air on Thursday. And they were!

Once our feelings changed around the timing of our vacation, everything aligned to create the ideal scenario. I watched in amazement as our desires unfolded right before our eyes. We can't take credit for the pilots going on strike. We held true to our desire to avoid leaving our new business. We needed to stay in town, and that's what we did.

Who Murdered My Sister?
I hear you

Life is always answering my questions, and prayers.

Oh, how I love rainy days in Los Angeles. I love the day after a good rain even more because the air is crisp and the sky is clear, with picturesque views of the hills. This is one of the many reasons I love living in Los Angeles—this wonderful backdrop inspires me to dream a bigger dream.

For the last week, I had been thinking of my beloved sister, who made her transition some years ago at the hands of a perpetrator. She was murdered! It was more than thinking, it was a feeling. I could feel her, and she was on my mind and in my space even more than usual. It was consuming most of my day and I kept wondering, "What are you trying to tell me?" It was nonstop because the feelings were so strong. I began to ask questions. Again, I asked, "What are you trying to tell me? Who did this? Who is responsible for your death?" It was something I could not turn off; I could only ride the wave, staying open so I could receive the answer.

How could I pass the time that day? I could reorganize the store. It didn't take long to replenish the floor. What would I do with the other eight and a half hours of my ten-hour day? I could enjoy the rain, the fresh air, and do a little people watching; maybe try on a few new pieces? I decided to stay busy until the midday person came in and I would have someone to talk to.

"What is it? What are you trying to tell me? I do love and miss you, big sister. I know you're here, I know you are trying to tell me something! Who's responsible?" The thoughts came back! I didn't mind the recurring thoughts and feeling; I knew something was happening. "I know you're trying to tell me something. I know it was your time to go. I know it doesn't matter in which way you choose to make your transition. I know this, but as for everyone else, that's another story."

I have never known such pain as when I watched our mom fall apart, knowing she would never be the same. Our lives were changed forever. I thought I had some understanding of spirituality. I don't believe in death. Are we not spiritual beings having a physical experience? This concept is tossed about in religious teachings with little question as to its true meaning. As a child, I was very inquisitive; I wanted answers and I wasn't taking anyone's word for anything. I remember being maybe five years old, sitting on the toilet with my feet dangling as I contemplated life. Where did I come from? Who's moving my hand? I'm not a robot, so who's moving my hand? Looking at the back of my hand then the other side, I remembered getting an image of space that I now know is the universe.

The first time I went to church, I watched the pastor speak and thought to myself, "If God talks to him, why wouldn't he talk to me?" In my environment, religion was talked about in passing. My mother flirted with the idea of becoming a Jehovah's Witness for a while, and I would pick up bits and pieces about religion. One concept comes to mind: reincarnation. I had figured it out before the age of ten and have only since then confirmed what I knew to be true through common sense.

I thought about Jesus being so evolved and having the strength and courage to turn the other cheek. Now the thought of being Christ like permeated my mind. I became filled with the desire to know. That is a hard act to follow, walking on water, parting the sea, healing the sick . . . the list goes on. The next thought was, "What if you die when you're thirty? I'm sure thirty years is not enough time to become Christ like. What if you die at two years old?" It didn't make sense to me; I was sure that two years is not enough time. Then it hit me: you get to come back! This is the only logical answer. From that moment forward, I was clear: we come back again and again until we become Christ like.

I found myself standing in front of my family talking about my sister and what she means to me, and how I feel much closer to her now than ever before. As I looked around the church I was confused; why was my family crying? Intellectually, I knew the answer, but from a spiritual perspective, it didn't register. All I had learned about death and spirit wouldn't let me experience her as gone. Somewhere inside me, it is true, she is not dead. This feeling was more powerful, more real, than anything else. It was too strong to ignore. I felt at ease, peaceful in the mist of such agony and grief. It was as if I was in a bubble of complete love that allowed me to surrender and share from the deepest part of my being, remembering my big sister, celebrating her life and the beauty she brought to my world.

I digress. I noticed a familiar face across the street, a man who had been in the store on a number of occasions but never purchased anything. He would walk around the store looking at a few shirts, never trying on anything, and out he went just as fast as he entered. I don't think I'd ever heard him speak; he would give a nod to say hello. I could see his mouth moving but hardly a sound would come out. His demeanor was different when he was with his friend; he was often smiling, listening intently and taking in every detail of the story. From his expressions I could tell he was interested and wanted to hear more.

At first, I was a bit suspicious of his behavior as he walked around looking at a few pieces and then walked out. This had been his routine for quite some time. The clothes we sold in the store were a little flashy, not his style. Maybe that's why he headed to the back and looked at the light-weight jackets and gym attire. In any case, I kept an eye on him when he came in to browse.

I sometimes saw him and his friend jaywalking from the gym to their car in the grocery store's parking lot above my store. His friend was a little more outgoing and was usually trying to pick up girls in the neighborhood, something you don't see on a regular basis in the middle of West Hollywood. He was as tactful as a stray dog in heat running wild in the streets. My coworker and I thought it was quite comical, and she had sometimes been on the receiving end of his antics.

Their friendship struck me as odd; this guy was nothing like his friend. This fact alone made him more appealing. I would often take notice of him; it didn't matter what I was doing, it seemed as if I would look up at the right time to see them walking across the street or just passing the window. I think I had a little crush on him; there was something mesmerizing about him. I watched him whenever he was around. It's not as if he made a spectacle of himself like his buddy, but there was this connection I felt towards him. He dropped by the store occasionally to look at our clothing, which was strange, because he was always dressed in the same black sweats with a double white line on both sides of the leg and an oversized t-shirt; not very fashionable. Our store specializes in fashion-forward men's clothing that capitalized on the cotton/spandex blend popular in WeHo.

This young man had honey brown skin, wavy black hair that cascaded just past his shoulders, and a mustache. He looked about 5'10 and had a slender build and relatively small facial features, with the exception of beautiful, big brown eyes. His nose was narrow, well-proportioned for his oblong face. He had a very Middle Eastern appearance. I thought he was a nice-looking young man.

Now, all of a sudden, he was coming into my store. What would I do? I didn't think we've been alone before. There were usually two people in the store whenever I'd seen him, or he'd come in with his friend. Now it was just the two of us, no coworker, no friend, and no other customers. He walked in and I said hello. He acknowledged me by looking in my direction. I watched him walk back to his usual spot at the back of the store. I tried to look busy, I didn't ask if he needed help or if he was looking for something in particular. I said nothing, I looked out the window. Within moments he came up to the counter with a sweat jacket and a shirt. I was caught off guard because he'd never purchased anything before. He put the clothes on the counter but was looking down as he reached for his credit card and identification. I take his credit card and ID and he looked at me trying not to be noticed. I read his name and was shocked— JAMES ROBERSON! I thought to myself, "No way! No way!"

I remained calm as I handed James Roberson his credit card and ID. He mumbled something, I assumed it was, "Have a nice day," or "I love you," or "Goodbye," I couldn't be too sure. After James Roberson left, I stood there dumbfounded. Everything started to make sense, and now I knew why I'd had the feelings of my sister, the questions the thoughts and feelings of her being in my space. I don't know which came first: my questions or the feeling of her being with me which prompted the inquiry.

The name James Roberson was very significant to me. It was the name of the man accused of murdering my sister, who was found not guilty. James Roberson and this man, I had been admiring for months, had the exact same name! What were the chances? Coincidence? I don't think so. I had been infatuated with the young man for months. It wasn't something I wanted to pursue, but there was enough there to keep me interested. Would I have noticed his name had I not taken an interest in him? Would I have noticed him if I didn't find him attractive?

Everything was aligned perfectly, down to this very transaction, so I might have the answer I sought. This had started months prior to the feelings and thoughts around my sister. The universe's timing is impeccable; had anything been different, I would have missed the answer to my question. Of course, James Roberson is a common name, but the person with the name is anything but common. I don't remember James Roberson much more after that . . . I didn't have the interest anymore. It's possible I could have seen him again after that powerful experience, but nothing stands out. It was never about him.

I Am The Manifester

I have my answer, and that is enough for me. Thank you, my dear sweet sister, for answering my prayer again.

I know I have the answer to my question. Did my sister come to tell me the answer? Did I call her forth and get the answer I had known all along? In any case, I can put this question to rest. I am grateful for the signs she gave me that lead me to my truth. It was more of a confirmation.

A Trip to the Post Office
I need to buy stamps

I know I'm in the right place by the way I feel.

I was writing out my bills when I realized I needed stamps. I knew I would be going to the post office. I made my way there and purchased two stamps for the letters I had with me. I thought to buy the stamps as I walked out without them; I was preoccupied with the feeling that I should send something more to New Jersey. I had just sent a package to a friend there.

I got to work and the thoughts flowed freely. What more could I send? I wanted to send something useful. I went back and forth between sending and not sending something more. I knew if I was going to send something it would be on Tuesday, because I wanted the packages to arrive together on Wednesday.

I was at work on Tuesday with the dilemma at the forefront of my mind when I came up with the perfect gift. I knew my friend would be working on his first book, so I decided to send him a journal and cool pencils to show my support. I felt good about my decision and left for the post office again. On the way to my car, a guy stopped me to say hello. We made small talk and I decided to go by the bank before the post office. Although the post office is five minutes from my work place, I was taking a new route there. I headed out, and within a couple of turns I was there.

I was surprised, and thought to myself, "Wow, that was fast!" I made my way into the circular driveway and was about to turn into the parking lot when I noticed the car in front of me getting the first parking space. I hoped there would be another one.

I saw someone walking to his car on the opposite side of the parking lot just as the first car pulled in and I noticed another space next to it. I pulled into this spot and was grateful for it. I got out and the first thing I noticed was a book of stamps on the ground beside my car. A full book of stamps! Now I didn't have to purchase any . . . I looked at everything that got me to that very spot to get the parking space to get the book of stamps.

Everything lined up so that I might pull into the parking space. What timing and effortlessness on my part. I know that when I am loving and lighthearted, I am always in the right place at the right time. It is the feeling of love and peace that inspires me to action.

I Know What I Know
Every time I…

I am the manifester of my desires.

The universe never questions our desires; by our words are we justified. A roommate of mine used to say, "Every time I think I'm getting ahead, something happens. As soon as things are going well, when I have a little money something happens." I remember being in the car with him and I could feel he believed this to be the truth. More importantly, he had the proof. In the time that we lived together he was in five car accidents, and each time he would repeat, "I told you. It always happens!"

I can only imagine the feeling that arises in him when he thinks he's getting ahead. I'm sure he's looking for the thing that will prove his case, and like clockwork he is right. There is always something, because he expects there to be.

May this be a clear example that you get what you expect. He had the proof to back up his theory, and so it was. Let goodness flow forth in all areas of your life. Give little or no attention to the things you're wanting to move away from. Offer new energy to life, into the thing you desire to experience. Remember the truth of who you are by learn-

ing from your experience. Look deeper, feel the truth of why you may expect the worse. From this place think a new thought and notice the universe's response to what your new expectations are.

The Eleventh Hour
The universe has impeccable timing

I trust myself, I trust my feelings.

I was doing freelance decorating, the rent was due and I was two hundred and thirty-seven dollars short. I knew things would unfold as they should. I had a few days before the first of the month. I had two questions. The first was, "What will I say to my landlord?" The second was, "Where can I get the extra money?" Neither one felt good. I could call my client, who at the time had an outstanding debt. I knew what to do but I wasn't comfortable asking my client. I felt uneasy, I had a feeling of desperation—I just didn't feel right asking.

It was the last minute and I still had not mentioned the outstanding debt. We were getting together in the next two weeks and I had a few more things I needed to get for her bathroom before my work would be complete. She had offered to pay me last week and I'd told her I could wait until the job was finished. I think this is more of the feeling because I'd told her it would be okay to pay me in a couple of weeks. I didn't feel right putting her on the spot and the feeling of desperation was too much. I thought to call my landlord to tell him I would pay the balance in a few days. I knew in my heart that it wouldn't be a problem, because I had never been late with my rent before, and at one point I had paid my rent two months in advance. I had a good track record with my landlord, I knew he trusted me. I also knew the excitement in his voice when he collected rent. It made me feel good, knowing we were helping each other. He was helping me by renting the place to me, for which I was truly grateful. And I was helping him by showing my appreciation and gratitude by paying my rent on time.

The bottom line was that I was not going to put my client in the middle of my issue. Once I decided to surrender, I didn't want to think of some excuse as to why I would be a few days late on my rent. It would be the truth, but I didn't feel right calling to say so. More importantly, I didn't want to break my clean record. I had been there almost three years and had not been late once. Now I felt at ease, knowing things would work out.

Two hours later I decided to go to the supermarket, and on my way home, I had a feeling to get a lottery ticket. To my surprise, I won the exact amount I needed to pay my rent: two hundred and forty dollars. I remember feeling humbled by the experience and reminded again that I need only trust.

For a moment, I was willing to try and figure something out. I didn't like the feelings that accompanied this idea. I was aware of the discomfort in my body and decided to surrender. The moment I let go, I knew everything would be okay. It didn't matter; the feeling of peace reinforced my decision to trust. The feeling of peace is priceless. I witnessed another miracle by tuning into the truth of who I am and listening to my inner guidance. Although I had no ideas about how it would be resolved, what I did know was that it would all work out just fine, and it did with grace.

Makeover
Linen pants

I see what I desire to experience.

I had been thinking of getting a pair of white linen pants. One day, I noticed a woman wearing a pair similar to what I had in mind. She was some distance away and I didn't think to ask her about them, but I did make a mental note. The ideal pair was wide-legged with plenty of fabric, and looked like a long skirt at first glance. My intention was clear and I mentioned the idea to a few people. I was eager to devise a plan as to how I might find such a pant.

That same day, I was walking towards the front of the store in which I worked and a client came in wearing white linen pants—the very ones I wanted. I explained my desire and she said, "I have had these for more than two years." I said, "if this is the case, they have held up beautifully." I could not believe she walked in with the pants I was getting. It turned out the store from where she'd purchased them was around the corner from where I lived, at Hari Natural Fabric and Clothing. I couldn't wait to stop on my way home. When I got there I saw it was all linen clothing, mostly for women, but they told me it was unisex. The store specialized in a few simple patterns with ninety percent of the inventory linen and the rest cotton—a perfect store for linen lovers such as myself. I purchased three pairs of pants: white, sage, and khaki. I purchased two cotton shirts, very stylish with a bohemian influence. The shirts were one size, with script and images of Ganesh, Buddha, and the Om symbol in red and black. The cut was the same as a dashiki. Although the shirts were made of cotton, they were very lightweight, almost sheer. Definitely not something I could wear in the winter. It was nice for the beach or a day about town in a pair of old jeans; my favorite.

"I need to find a nice pair of linen pants," is a passing thought I had a few days prior to my client walking in. That very day, I was talking about it with a coworker. The idea was at the forefront of my mind. I am open to seeing signs leading to my heart's desires. I allow the universe to do what it does best—make it happen! I only need to hold my attention long enough to evoke some excitement around the thing, and experience what I wish to call forth.

Ask and You Shall Receive
Sewing Machine

Life gives me what I ask for.

I needed a heavy-duty sewing machine. I'd talked to Naomi about getting an older machine, and she reminded me of the importance of having a professional machine for the type of sewing I would be doing. After a week or two she brought the subject up again. I said, "The next time you are out, keep your eyes open for a machine." Now the ball was in motion. Meanwhile, I spoke to my friend Camille about my desire for an old machine. She mentioned her days back in Jamaica sewing for her family, making her siblings' and later her kids' clothes. The machine she used then was still in working order; she had promised it to a friend some time ago and the friend had not come to collect the machine. We talked about my other decorating projects and went about our day. I must add that Camille is very supportive. I remember this most: she really believed in me and my dreams of making window treatments.

A few weeks later, I was talking with Camille and she said she had a gift for me. I had forgotten about the sewing machine. She said, "I know what you are wanting to do, I know this will help you in your business."

Camille brought the machine with her and offered it to me. I mentioned the woman that was coming to get it, and she said that if she'd really wanted it, she would have come to pick it up. I was very grateful and I offered to pay her, but she wouldn't have it. She asked that I pursue my dreams. What a lovely gesture. I have the sewing machine today and I am still making window treatments for myself and a few close friends.

It is amazing how simple it is to get the things I need. The same process applies for every area of my life. I am willing to take a close look at my life and think a new thought. If I am not satisfied by my experiences I will offer a new thought, a new idea, a bigger dream, or a better ending to my story. I have experienced enough to know better. To know the power is in my hands.

Harmonious Home
Right sized plants

*I am at peace, I trust my first thought,
it is the right one.*

I wanted living plants in my home. I needed some greenery, so I went to Home Depot to find my two houseplants. They did have Philodendrons in four-inch pots, but they were not the right size for me. I wanted them larger; I had seen them before with much bigger leaves. I left thinking, "Where might I find them?" I thought about going downtown to check out the flower district.

The following week I had the idea to go downtown, but I wasn't up for the drive. I wanted to go check out some fabric for another project and I could look for the plants then, but I couldn't bring myself to get in the car. I used excuses such as, "It's too late to drive downtown." The thought then came to me to go back to Home Depot again. More excuses: "You were just there and they didn't have the plant you wanted in the right size!" But the idea wouldn't leave, so I decided to drive back to the store. I got there and to my surprise, there were two overgrown plants, just as I had imagined them on my first trip to the store! They were in the same place as the two I had seen last week. I smiled and said, "Thank you!" and brought them home.

I Am The Manifester

I wanted the plant with the larger leaves. It turned out they would be there on my second visit. The thought was clear to go back to Home Depot. My logical mind reminded me of my trip earlier that week. I was sure the plants would not be there. I gave in to the feeling, trusted my feeling and made the second trip. The plants were hanging in the same place as the smaller ones had been. Now that I think about it, the smaller ones were gone. I was happy to find the right-sized plants.

I Love What I Do
Taking pride in my work

I am looking forward to the ideal outcome.

I was in a new city and in search of someone to braid my hair. I knew the importance of seeing someone's work before trusting them with my hair. I once made the mistake of just going to a braider on the word of someone I hardly new. I remember the girl being a bit young to be doing my braids, but you never know. She had a friend come by to help with my hair, her friend seemed to be around the same age. If I were to guess their ages, they would be between seventeen and twenty-one. I had a young lady braid my hair before and she was amazing; she wanted to open her own salon. With this girl, though, I think she was in it for a quick buck. I could feel by the sections and the speed with which she was doing my hair that it was not what I wanted. I didn't leave, though, because I had nowhere else to go. I didn't know anyone else so I was stuck; I would have to wait it out. When they were done, the sections in my hair were huge... HUGE I tell you! I went home to take them out. It was a horrific experience. I was more upset at myself for not stopping her and saying it wasn't right than at her for being wrong. It wasn't so much her as it was me not listening to myself.

There is an art to great hair braiding. It's something that comes with years of practice, a love for the art of braiding, and patience. If the braider is in a hurry, forget about it. I have experienced my share of bad braiders. I once went to a friend of a friend to have my hair done, and even though we'd had a few consultations and I thought she understood what I wanted, I could tell while she worked on my hair that she was not clear about what she was doing. I asked again if it would be full and in the style I desired, the style we had discussed. She assured me it would be, and I trusted her because she told me she knew what she was doing. There were moments during the first consultation when I could feel myself not believing what she said, and I questioned her about it a few times, asking, "Are you sure this is the right hairstyle for me?" "Yes!" she responded with confidence (or was it arrogance?). I knew better! When it comes to this particular hairstyle, I could do it myself, but I wasn't in the mood to do it. I wanted to have someone do my hair.

As she was finishing my hair, I could feel it was not turning out the way we had discussed, and she was stalling, trying to figure out what her next move would be. It was as if she was in a chess game and was destined to lose. Time was up, I had to get to work. It looked horrible, but there was nothing I could do! I left and thanked her for trying and never looked back. My hair was all over my head; I looked like Macy Gray gone wild. I put on a bandana and went to work. I never said a word to my friend, but vowed that the next time I would go to another hair stylist, I would have my hair braided the right way. I did, and it looked fabulous, if I do say so myself. I didn't say anything about that nightmare nor did my friend.

I thought of the idea of finding a great braider. I held this intention on a daily basis. I knew someone would show up. I remember walking into work and passing a girl who had her hair in nice braids. I thought to myself, "Her hair looks nice, but not quite what I'm looking for." I gave thanks to my angels and the universe for listening to me and bringing forth choices. Later that week a woman came to see me and her hair was braided flawlessly; it was absolutely beautiful. I asked her where she had them done and who was her stylist, and she responded that she'd had them done in Africa. Wow, it looked great! But I can't go to Africa just to get my braids done. I told her I was looking for someone to do my braids. Elizabeth told me she knew of someone locally that does an incredible job, the woman who does her hair when she isn't in Africa. I asked if I could have her number. I was very excited because I could tell Elizabeth knew what great braids looked like; she was the ideal person to lead me to the perfect stylist. This woman's hair was so finely braided, the smallest braids I've seen in quite some time.

Most importantly, the thing I asked for was now in my experience. My new stylist's name is Lily, and she is remarkable. My hair is beautiful, it's perfect—and get this: she is from Africa. It goes to show me that the universe is always conspiring with me to give me what I tune in to.

I would see people with their hair braided and I would think "It's good, but not the one." I knew my prayers were being answered. I made a mental note of the right-sized braid and the style. I knew it would be something I would feel the moment I encountered the right person. The day Elizabeth walked into my work place, it was an instant knowing. It's been more than a year and I am still satisfied with my braider. She continues to amaze me with her consistency.

Fearless Faith
I am unstoppable

I am open to abundance in every way.

March of 2008 is a month I will never forget. I had reached the end of my rope, as far as my children were concerned. I had been without transportation for the last three years. I would get rides to the doctor and the grocery store, and any other errands I may need to attend to. I was now at the mercy of my kids, friends, and sometimes public transportation. I was done! I didn't have the energy to ask over and over again for one more favor from my kids. I was tired of the excuses; I was tired of feeling like a burden to my children.

After sulking for an entire weekend, I awoke on Monday with a new attitude and determination. I called my daughter one last time to ask if she could take me to a car dealership. "I am buying a truck!" I announced. She said, "I have something to do, but I can drop you off. Why are you going to the car dealer? Do you have money for a truck?" I responded, "No!" She asked, "How are you going to get a car without a down payment, without any money?" I didn't have a response.

When I got to the car dealership, a salesman came and asked, "How may I help you?" I said, "I want to buy a truck." He asked, "How much do you have to put down as a down payment?" I said, "Nothing." I didn't have any money for a down payment. He then asked, "Do you have good credit?" I said, "No, I do not." He was kind enough to tell me what I would need to get a truck and sent me on my way. I did not give up. I walked to another dealership, where the salesman asked the same questions and had a similar attitude.

When I arrived at dealership number three, I was ready for the standard questions, and to him I would have the same replies. "How much money do you have to put down?

"None!"

"Do you have good credit?"

"NO!"

"What is it you do for work?"

"Nothing. I don't have a job!"

The salesman was now a bit puzzled. He asked, "How do you intend to pay for this truck?" I said, "I intend to collect scrap metal." The salesman asked if I could call him back in a couple of days; he needed to go to the auction to look for a truck that would suit my needs. I was somewhat comfortable about his proposal, but I did have my doubts. A couple of days passed and I had not called him; to my surprise, I received a phone call from him. He asked if I could come back to the dealership that Friday at 11:00. I was skeptical; I wasn't sure if he was pulling my leg, so I didn't go. He called to ask, "What happened? Why did you not show up?"

"I am sorry, but I didn't think you were going to give me a truck, considering that I don't meet any of the requirements," I answered.

He asked, "When can you get here?"

"It will take a couple of hours because I have to walk there." He asked, "Where are you?" I gave him directions and he picked me up within an hour.

Once we arrived at the dealership, he pointed out the truck and asked if I would like to take it for a test drive. It was a white four-door pick-up truck, more than I had imagined. I was in love! I was in my truck! It was a feeling of joy, freedom and complete bliss! I could do what I wanted—this was freedom!

I went into his office and filled out the necessary paperwork. The salesman was not only gracious, but he was also the owner. It was truly my lucky day. He said, "You know, you can't drive the truck off the lot without insurance." I must have had a blank look on my face because he asked, "Now what's wrong?" I said, "I don't have money for insurance." He made some phone calls and got a company to sign me, then took out his credit card to pay for it. To say I was speechless would be an understatement. Everything was falling into place as if orchestrated by the heavens. I now believe that its the only way; I found myself in the right place at the right time. I had the truck and it was time to leave the lot, but I had no money for gas, and yes... you guessed it, he gave me twenty-five dollars to get gas. I was off to work. I had made fifty dollars within a hour, and to top it off, the insurance company came by to take pictures of the truck and gave me a gas voucher for twenty-five dollars. I was later told by the finance company that I had two months before my first payment was due. Now that's magic!

It is a knowing that comes over me when I move without fear, and trust. I did have moments of doubt but I continued to go with it. I knew it was meant to be! I have had the truck for more than two years now, and I have one year left to pay for it in full. I am good friends with the owner. I call him up from time to time to say hello. I have sent quite a few people to him for vehicles.

We Love Entertaining
Party planner

I now let the universe take care of the details.

I love hosting Christmas parties and holiday gatherings. I will use almost any excuse to decorate. I love party planning. I wanted to update our kitchen with stainless steel appliances, and I mentioned this to my husband. He thought it was a nice idea, but "It's not in the budget, hon." This did not deter me from my desires. I had gotten the idea to create a vision book, so I found a picture of the appliances I wanted and put them in my book. I wasn't fixated on the images, but it was at the forefront of my mind from time to time.

It was business as usual, I was at work and I got a frantic call from my son. He was crying uncontrollably and I asked him, "What's wrong? Are you ok?"

He said, "I burned down the kitchen."

I asked again, "Are you all right?" I assured him that everything would be ok. Once I got over the initial shock of knowing that my child could have been seriously injured, I asked what happened.

"I wanted to make some shrimp. I saw you cooking some last night and thought I would make some for myself today. I put the skillet on the stove and put some oil in the pan. I turned the stove on and went to do more homework. I got sidetracked and noticed light flashing on the wall. I thought, 'What is that?' I jumped up to investigate and that's when I saw the kitchen on fire. The cabinets were melting and dark smoke was everywhere. I had a water bottle and tried to douse the flames but it didn't work! I started to panic because I didn't think I would be able to put the fire out. I grabbed the hose from the kitchen sink and continued to spray the fire until it went out. The range had melted, the kitchen was covered in black smoke and soot. The fire alarm was going off, it was a nightmare."

I assured my son that everything would be just fine. I asked if he had called his father, and he said yes. I told him I would talk to him later, but before getting off the phone, I said, "Thank you for my new kitchen!"

I would never want to put anyone in harm's way to manifest my desires, especially my children. It was within six months that I first mentioned to my husband about upgrading the kitchen. My son wasn't aware of my plans to remodel the kitchen or my desire to get new appliances. This happened the day before his sixteenth birthday. I now ask for my desires to come under grace.

Gracious Living
Love at first sight happens more times than not

I now let the universe take care of the details.

I was invited to the studio of a client whose specialty was window treatments. I walked into a well-designed space with twelve-foot ceilings. Sheer off-white fabric was draped from ceiling to floor dividing the room. I later found out the work space was on the other side of the curtain, a wonderful idea that makes great use of the space. The studio had a round table with four oversized plush chairs, all covered in an orange and white pattern, a very popular design at the time. Each chair had a skirt with inverted pleats in front and back, a thing of beauty. My focus was on the chairs; I was all about them, I wanted to know where she had found them. I sat in awe, caressing the sides of the chair and admiring the great craftsmanship. I was in heaven. The client said she found them in a second-hand store for twenty-five dollars per chair. GET OUT! She assured me it was the price and I asked, "Was it a mistake?" She said, "I wasn't waiting around to find out." I asked, "Where is this place?" She gave me directions and I was loving the chairs even more. They looked like recliners in size, but they were covered in gorgeous fabric. They looked a little like wingback chairs without the wings. I wanted to end the conversation and go to this store to see what more they might have, so we finished our meeting and made plans for me to come by her home studio.

After a month or so, I visited her home work space, and as I walked into the living room, the four chairs were there. She said that things hadn't worked with her and her partner. "I think these chairs are too big for my space, and I remembered how much you loved them. Would you like two?" I couldn't get the word out fast enough: "Yes! Are you sure?" She said yes, she didn't have the space for all four. I was in disbelief. I had two of the chairs I was loving and appreciating. I did think it would be great to have all four, but I didn't want to be greedy. I set out to get them re-upholstered. I wanted my new chairs covered in purple, so I went looking for the ideal fabric.

I was freelancing as a decorator and was looking for chairs and other jewels for my clients, and I had gotten into the groove of finding the most amazing chairs. The client that gave me the chairs made a remark about me having a love affair with chairs. I hadn't thought about it, so I decided to count the chairs I had accumulated, and it turned out that I had thirteen chairs just for me—not including the chairs I had found for my clients along the way. Now I am a bit more aware when I'm out shopping. I give it a second thought before choosing a chair.

One day I was in another second-hand store and I noticed two small club chairs with round backs, with a dark cherry-wood stain and small gold studs around the frame. Very cute chairs for ten dollars; can't beat that. I called my client and told her of my incredible find. The chairs would need to be re-upholstered unless my client liked burnt orange. She said to bring them by, she couldn't wait to see them. I made my way to her house on the other side of town, excited to share my chairs. I took them out of the back seat and she ran out to have a look. We sat in her front yard talking in the new chairs. I could see she really liked them, so we took them inside to see how they looked there. We sat and talked a little more before the question came. "I need to ask you a question, and I need you to be honest with me. I need you to tell me the truth." I had no idea where she was going with this line of questioning until she said, "Do you like these chairs?" I interrupted her and said, "No, you like them!" She said, "I am wondering if you want to exchange these chairs for the other two chairs."

What? I could not believe what I was hearing. From my initial attraction and appreciation and love for those chairs, from first glance to the thought of having all four, to having an opportunity to have them in my possession; it was too much to take in! I could only respond, "Yes!" The beauty is that she loved those chairs as much as I loved the others. We were both happy.

Is it possible that in my love affair I was attracting the right chairs for my client so that she would have the same appreciation and fondness as I did for her four chairs? This is the part about the universe that left me speechless. I could not have set out to orchestrate such a turn of events so that I might have the things I appreciated so much in the first moments of seeing them. It's love and oneness that brought the chairs into my life. Is it really that simple? I say yes, it is. Take a moment and look at your life and see the things you have manifested just by appreciating them and loving them just as they are, with complete acceptance.

The things I love are aligned with me before I am consciously aware of them. It is in the moment of appreciation that I make my dreams come true. I had enough love to manifest the chairs, not ones like them, but the same chairs. I never had to ask. My client's words were, "I know how much you love them." She noticed my appreciation and remembered it and offered two chairs to me. Again—my thought was to have four chairs, the full set, and now I do. I appreciated these chairs into my life by loving them completely. I know this pulled them into my life, allowing me to experience them fully.

I Healed Myself
Laughter is the best medicine

*I tuned into the end result, holding clear vision,
loving every moment, knowing that I am healed.*

When I went to a medical clinic to have an ear infection checked on, I was shocked to hear that my platelet count was 146,000, which is below the healthy count of 150,000 to 450,000 platelets. (Platelets are the cells that help to clot the blood.) A few days later, the doctors at the medical center told me that my count had decreased to 120,000. Their plan was to prescribe medicine for me to take for the rest of my life, as this low platelet condition, thrombocytopenia, is not known to be reversible, and it could present danger if I were cut or in an accident. Before they prescribed any medicine, I told them that I was determined to take a few weeks to find another way to increase my platelet count.

From my psychology and spiritual studies, I know that the mind and body and spirit all work together, and that can affect my body with what I think, what I do, and how I feel. Though I didn't fully believe that I could make blood platelets with my thoughts, I wanted to try. During my meditation, I had a thought that I could make platelets by dancing and singing. I wasn't sure of the idea, so I consulted with a medical intuitive for guidance on next step. She told me that I already had an idea about what to do, and if I would do that, then I would heal the condition. She specifically stated that, for this situation, I could reverse the condition without the medicine of Western doctors. That phone session with her helped me believe in my abilities to co-create more platelets.

For the next two weeks, my daily routine was like the staging of a musical production about making blood platelets! When I awoke in the mornings, I would sing to myself, "I'm making plaaaatelets." The goofiness of it made me smile, and I continued through the day. Breathe in... making platelets. Breathe out... making platelets. If I told someone of my low platelet condition, I would also tell them, "Right now, I'm making platelets, lots and lots of platelets!" I asked my friends to please pray for me to help me make even more platelets.

Twice a day, I would dance around the living room for fifteen minutes, usually with my daughter. We would hold hands, twirl, and sing, "Platelets, platelets, Mommy's making platelets." For our free-style dancing, I played up-tempo classical marches, world music, and Celtic bagpipe music, because I felt invigorated by them. I howled, clapped, and cheered encouragement to myself as I moved.

From March 14 to April 4 of 2003, my platelet count rose from 120,000 to 138,000 and further increased to 146,000 in another two weeks. I continued to raise my platelet count and maintained a healthy level. I have not forgotten the power of music and song and dance and affirmative phrase. I continue to enjoy spicing up my daily routine with dancing and singing and affirmations, as well as sharing these ideas with others.

The Big Apple
Window shopping

Appreciation brings the things I love into my experience.

A number of years ago, my daughter and I moved to New York City from Charleston, South Carolina. We moved on a shoestring budget and when we arrived in New York, we barely had the money to hire movers to empty our U-Haul. The crew that we found that fit our budget (and came with insurance!) was not available immediately, so we were put on a waiting list. During these few days, I pounded the pavement on a quest for work. One day, on Fifth Avenue down towards Union Square, I passed the most exquisite furniture shop. I was in absolutely no position to acquire anything, but the shop called me, and so in I went! One soft green velvet and tapestry sofa caught my attention immediately and I needed look no further. This was my dream couch. The price tag was in the thousands; hence it was truly to remain a dream.

The next day the movers came to carry our belongings up the four flights of narrow, winding stairs. My sofa at the time was a large hide-a-bed, which was very heavy and once upon a time (prior to Hurricane Hugo, when it got drenched by plough mud), stunning. Now it was a shadow of its former self and retained some of the swampy odor. As the men tried to maneuver it around a corner on the third floor, one of them opened a window to allow for more leverage. Suddenly a foot slipped, so too the grip on the sofa, and OUT the window it flew!

A few weeks later the insurance company mailed us a check for a thousand dollars to compensate for our loss. With a spark to my step, I hot-footed it down to the little shop on Fifth Avenue, just to look. A sign in the window said "Clearance on all Floor Samples." There was my dream couch, waiting for me, marked down to $999.

Needless to say, I have luxuriated in my joy over this sofa for years, and it is still luscious.

I trusted my instincts; I'd thought I would just get a closer look at this beautiful work of art. I only appreciated it long enough for the universe to get a clear hit on my desires. This was another wonderful confirmation for me, a reminder to dream to love and appreciate life and the best the world has to offer.

part two
Manifesting Process

CLARITY
APPRECIATION
ALIGNMENT
ENERGETIC FOUNDATION
EXPECTANCY
WORDS AND AFFIRMATIONS
INTENTION
IMAGINATION
FEELING IT (KNOWING)
TRUST
SURRENDER (NO WORRIES)

Examples of the Manifesting Process In Action

This section gives clear examples of how you might use the formula. It can be applied to anything you believe is possible. I must add that it doesn't work on people! You can manifest the ideal mate for yourself, but a particular person... everyone has free will. Why waste time trying to get someone to love you who is not interested? For those of you who are looking for love, wouldn't it serve you and your potential lover, husband, wife, soul mate better if you did the necessary work to be the ideal partner? Remember, you can give what you don't have!

This formula gives you a step-by-step process of how to get from point A to point B. You may look at the stories and see which formula is used. You may not need to go from A-Z. As you will see in Jeffrey's story, he needed to trust and use words and affirmations. He also needed to surrender the hows.

May this be the start of a new life, a new journey. Have fun, be easy, and when in doubt, look to your life experiences. If that is not enough, look to the stories and process and affirmations. If you are willing, so too is the universe, willing and ready to support you in all you believe is possible. I don't have all the answers, but what I do know is that every story in this book is the truth. If nothing else, I am hopeful that we might reawaken to this power/force on a moment-to-moment basis, living a life of BLISS!

I shall see you on the other side of destiny.

Manifesting Process for Love

CLARITY

Step 1: If you believe in love, what does the best love relationship look like? Harmony, peace, support, integrity, compassion, and respect. These qualities must be something you embody, because like attracts like. Get clear about what you are wanting to experience. What does love look like? Look around at couples you admire and choose the best from those relationships. If there is no one around that you can admire, look around in your experience for evidence of what love looks like. Notice the way loving couples interact with one another. The way they look at one another. It is up to you to define what you are wanting to experience in your love relationship. You must be willing to tell a new story, one you wish to experience around love. The best you can imagine around love.

Manifesting Process For Love

Appreciation

Step 2: Start telling new stories around what you love about the idea of being in a romantic relationship. Look at couples and appreciate all you are wanting to experience. That which you are wanting to call forth, notice in every couple you see.

Make it a natural expression, not forced. It is something you notice. You appreciate it because it reminds you of what you desire to experience. The more you notice couples holding hands and being loving towards each other the better. Get inspired and know you are in the process of manifesting your own love relationship.

The more you can tune into this concept, the closer you are to having the love you are desiring. If you are already in a love relationship, what could you appreciate about your partner or yourself for being with the person you are loving? What could you appreciate about the relationship? If you wish to remain in the relationship, it will be easy to find the goodness, the things you appreciate about being in love. Remember to always look for more of what you desire to experience.

Alignment

Step 3: Get into alignment with love, the love relationship you are wanting to experience. Watch movies about love that have happy endings. Choose movies that bring about feelings of romantic hope and inspiration. Be excited about manifesting the love of your life. Start to think that you are preparing for your ideal mate. I often say to women that Mr. Right is not looking to fix you! Consider the degree to which you have gone to meet a man or a woman. Maybe you've been calling him or her Mr. or Mrs. Right. Rarely have I met someone who truly prepares for what they want; more often than not, they are settling for less than they deserve. Write a list of the characteristics of the ideal person for you. Now that you have the clear image of this ideal person, remember that like attracts like, even in the notion of opposites attract. You can write love letters to your love. The more you are in tune with this feeling, the sooner you will have someone to share them with.

ENERGETIC FOUNDATION

Step 4: Energetic foundation is having a feeling and knowingness that it's happening. When you are in a place of excitement, when you no longer notice your immediate situation and you are focused on your desires, you are now celebrating your life as it is. You will know you are worthy of a loving relationship. In this experience, you are at ease around love. When you have done steps one and two long enough, you will be in a feeling of joy and excitement. When you are no longer concerned about the outside world, when you are not needing the opinions and approval of your friends or the world, you will know that you are in the full experience of your energetic foundation. The proof is in your feelings, and that is enough. You are love, and therefore love shows up from a place of confidence. Now you are standing on solid ground, feeling loved, lovable and loving.

EXPECTANCY

Step 5: What are you expecting? Are you halfheartedly moving through these exercises? If so, you will feel similar to the energy you are offering. You must expect to see signs of your desires coming forth. The truth of the matter is that you are getting what you expect. Actually, all that you are experiencing is what you've expected, in one form or another. If you are taking the time to do this, why not put forth the effort to expect the best-case scenario? You are now tuned into love and the good feelings that are evoked from doing these exercises. If you are doing the exercises as suggested, you will feel a shift in your energy. You will move to a place of belief. Now expect your desires to be! The love you are seeking is seeking you, and you are needing to expect a new experience around love by expecting it.

Do you expect to meet your soul mate? Are you expecting to meet a different caliber of person? Someone who has the same values, with integrity, compassion, and humility? A person more aligned with your desires? Are you looking forward to manifesting the ideal husband or wife for yourself, by your own standards. Follow this formula and you will offer something more to the universe—a new request.

Words and Affirmations

Step 6: Use your words to change your life. You have used them to create the life you see before you now. If you are not satisfied with your life, choose new words to tell a new story. Find words that bring about good feelings around love. What could you say that is positive about a new love relationship? What words could you use to give you hope? Refer to the Affirmations section of this book to find an affirmation around love that inspires you. Start to pay attention to your words. You could be making this process easy or more challenging, depending on the words you choose. Make every statement around love be what you are wanting to experience, and watch your world unfold by the command of your words.

What loving words could you say to yourself on a daily basis? Consider "I am worthy of love." What if you use your words and affirmations to first change how you feel about yourself? I've spoken to many seeking love, and most are not doing the necessary work to be the healed person that would make for a healthier relationship. Mr. or Mrs. Right isn't going to stick around for long after the honeymoon phase. This is when you can no longer keep up the pretense, and the truth of who you are will surface. All the unhealed drama you've tried to cover up with hair color and lipstick or muscles and nice cars must come forth. Nothing is more powerful then love, self-love extended outward to manifest itself in the form of the ideal mate. This can never be replaced with pretense of any kind. The universe knows the truth of who you are; the only one you are fooling is yourself.

Now what words will you say to become your loving self? Be fearless when it comes to being your authentic self, and the universe will support you completely. Now get clear, get real, and get on with it!

Intention

Step 7: What are your intentions around love? Do you intend to experience love first for yourself, flowing through you? Are you intending to heal your past so you might love in a way you have never love before? Are you intending to love yourself first?

What is your intention for love? If you are more focused on feeling love first, you will have a clear idea of what you are deserving in a love relationship. It's important to state your intention on a daily basis. Each time you make such statements, it fuels your desires for the love you are manifesting. It's shifting your vibration and energy for the full experience of love as you've intended and so it is.

Trust

Step 8: When you are trusting that the love is here, then it will be. Trust is about having no worries! When you get to the place where you are no longer seeking love, it must come calling. If you have done this process, you must be feeling different about the idea of your love relationship. At this point, you must be in the place of hope, joy, and knowingness. It is a feeling in this step that will tune in to where you are. If you are worried, then you have more work to do. When you are in trust, it is just that.

When you trust, you are not looking for anything or anyone. You are loving life and living, being all you are meant to be. Without worrying, you look up and you're in love. Everything you've wanted is standing before you because you have done the work, and with the loving support of the universe it is done. The universe responds to the energy you offer in every moment, and now you are offering the energy of love, contentment, peace and well-being.

Imagination

Step 9: Let your imagination be free when thinking of love, being loved, and being loving. When you think of the ideal love relationship, if you have done step one on clarity, you should have clear visions of what you are wanting to experience. The more you flow with the images, the more images will come. If you can imagine it, it then becomes possible for you. When it comes to a particular person, do consider they have free will and may not have similar desires. It is best to have the ideal experience of your desires for love.

Without trying to make a particular person your love, trust the universe. It knows what is best for you, and the more clarity you offer, the better. You will begin to get clear images of heaven on earth. See yourself as you wish to be in this harmonious relationship. What are you doing? How do you feel, how do you look, what are you wearing? What's wonderful and amazing about you in this relationship?

Feeling it

Step 10: What does love feel like? How does it feel being in love? What does it feel like when you are loving towards yourself? You must be willing to feel yourself with the fullness of love—first for yourself! Do loving things with yourself. Say loving things to yourself. Treat yourself as you would want the ideal mate to treat you. I assure you that you are well on your way to experiencing the flow of love. If you can't feel it, use your words to shift your feelings. Say it over and over again. Choose an affirmation from the section for love and change how you feel about love.

Love must start from within! We are always attracting the equivalent of how we truly feel about ourselves in our work, friendships and love relationships. We can't give what we don't have, so we ask for one thing and get something else, or even its opposite. We are often looking for someone to make us feel like we're on the top of the world, but how can they if we don't feel we are deserving of such treatment? There is only truth in the universe, and your true feeling about a thing will be what you will call forth, what you manifest.

Surrender

Step 11: Surrender means knowing that you are love. You are worthy of love. When you are in a place of surrender, you are no longer looking outside yourself for this experience of love. When you are love, you notice loving things in the world. You do things in loving ways because it's flowing through you.

Our natural state is love. It is the truth of who we are—no more, no less. What else is there? Anything less than love is illusion!

Manifesting Process for Peace

CLARITY

Step 1: What is peace? What does peace mean to you? Is going for a walk peaceful? The idea is to take time to contemplate peace, to get clarity. Is being on the beach peaceful? Doing something you love could be peaceful. Consider being at peace as another form of peace. As you contemplate these ideas, you will start to get in tune with peaceful ideas for you. Being with the one you love, lying in their arms could be peaceful. Reading a good book can be peaceful. Sitting with yourself in the rest-room and taking a moment to breathe before going back into the meeting can create a peaceful disposition. The good news is that there are as many ways to experience peace as there are people, so have fun manifesting peace.

Some may think a quiet night at home is peaceful. Going for a swim, making dinner, just being in the moment and loving life as it is, can be peaceful. It matters not what is going on around you. Peace is a state of being—it's a decision you must make. Ask and you shall receive. Set your sight on peace in any given moment and show yourself the truth of who you are: a spiritual, manifesting being. If you are looking for peaceful work, imagine being in a state of peace while doing the thing you love, thus evolving into the perfect career.

APPRECIATION

Step 2: How might someone appreciate peace? If you are worried, anxious, or upset, you might appreciate peace. You might wish for it! Now would be the time to call forth moments of peace as you appreciate the past experiences of peace, or for the peace you are looking forward to. A peaceful vacation, the desire to be at home with your significant other could be peaceful. The purpose is to acknowledge peace, and your appreciation for it will call forth all sorts of ideas that will let you experience peace.

In times of stress you might appreciate a quiet night at home, a hot bath or shower. You might appreciate taking time to breathe and sitting in silence. Organizing your home, doing some project around your home may be peaceful. Once you have done something you have been putting off, this alone could put you in a state of peace.

ALIGNMENT

Step 3: Getting into alignment with peace. If you are taking a moment to breathe, you are in alignment with peace. If you are walking on the beach and noticing the beauty, peace must follow. If you are cuddling with your puppy, you are aligned with peace. If you are sitting in your favorite chair while reading a wonderful book, this could align you with peace.

If you are painting just because, this could align you with peace. When you are doing something you truly love, this too could align you with peace. If you are taking time to sit with yourself, this could align you with peace. When you let go of your need to be right, this could be very peaceful. Taking a meditation class, yoga, *tai chi*, being out in nature, a quiet dinner with friends, or reading a good book are other ways that you can experience peace.

Manifesting Process For Peace

Energetic Foundation

Step 4: Peace is a state of being, an experience. You must pay close attention to your feelings. I was speaking to a client once about a troubling situation, and she remarked that she already knew everything I was sharing with her, but that sometimes you must do something physical. I reminded her that when you are in peace, you are inspired to the physical action from a place of peace. One must be willing to see it as they desire it to be. I asked her to use affirmations, but she had little luck. It is safe to say that the experience did not unfold peacefully.

Expectancy

Step 5: What do you expect around peace? Are you expecting to have a peaceful outcome? Do you expect to encounter peaceful people while driving in rush hour traffic? Are you expecting your work environment to be peaceful? Try this one: are you expecting to respond in a peaceful manner? Do you consider yourself to be a peaceful person? Could your world be more peaceful? I tell you this, it will be, if you are expecting it to be peaceful!

Words and Affirmations

Step 6: What words could you use to experience peace? I am peaceful! Peace is the way to be. When I stop trying, I ride the wave of peace. Peace is a daily choice. When I am looking for peace, I always find it. You could also choose words that bring about a peaceful feeling. Beautiful nature walks. Floating in the pool on a nice sunny day. Having a romantic picnic. Holding hands with the love of your life. Sleeping in on a rainy day. Now you get the idea! Choose words and affirmations from the list in the Affirmations section of this book, under Peace. These are some words that may bring about peace: beauty, harmony, love, grace, and joy. What is peaceful to you? If you are not sure, ask yourself. The truth of who you are will oblige you with the answer.

INTENTION

Step 7: Is it your intention to be at peace? Do you intend to have a peaceful experience? Pay close attention to those moments when you are hoping for the best. Let's say that going to the DMV may be an all-day event. It is up to you to choose how you will respond to the possibility of waiting in line. If you are choosing to experience peace, you might ask yourself how waiting in line could be a peaceful experience. You can intend to be at peace. You could read a book, meet new people, catch up on your email, you could do a standing meditation with light breathing (you don't want to offend anyone). You could bless everyone you notice, sending a silent prayer. You could bless the experience and make somebody's day by choosing to be at peace. Intend to make the best out of every situation by intending peace.

IMAGINATION

Step 8: The act or power to form a mental image of something that is not present. Enough thinking had to have taken place in order for it to be in your experience. For example, what would you love to experience around peace? You could sit in your office at a job you are wanting to change, and imagine a more peaceful work place. If you are having to have a serious talk with someone, you could take a second and imagine it going peacefully. If you are in a noisy environment that you cannot escape, you can tune into a more peaceful experience. You could tune into peace and tune out noise. It is a willingness to experience peace using your imagination.

FEELING IT

Step 9: Feeling peaceful. Feeling is the best life has to offer. I say this because it is in your inner being that calls forth the feelings which bring about the experience. What could be more beautiful? If you think that you can't feel peace when you are worried about bills, I would suggest you think how you might feel after you have resolved the issue. Call forth the feelings of peace that you would feel once you knew things were working out. I know that once you find peace, you will soon feel peace, and have a desire to do something that may change everything.

Trust

Step 10: When you know that all is well, you trust! Trust is acting as if the end result is in your favor. It's knowing that whatever happens, everything will be ok—peaceful. Trust that the world is a peaceful place, and it will be. Does this concept fit peacefully in your belief system? With the notion of getting what you expect?

Although my client wanted peace, she wasn't willing to do more to get into a peaceful state. The fear around what could or would happen ruled her thinking, making for a huge distraction and taking her further away from a peaceful experience. You have the life that you are complaining about or dreaming about—it's your choice!

Surrender

Step 11: Surrender in peace. Now there's a concept! To surrender in peace is to move on, knowing that all is well. When you are at peace, surrendering is easy. Without worry you are moving forward and living life. When you truly surrender you've done all you could and let the universe handle the details. You might say, "It's out of my hands," and it is.

Manifesting Process for Money

Clarity

Step 1: Before you can manifest anything, you must get clear. If you have not decided what you want, you will get something similar to what you now have. This is true for every aspect of your life. If you are not taking the time to think a new thought about a thing, then how can it manifest? How can it change when you know how it's going to turn out, based on past experiences? Now what are you wanting to manifest as far as money?

If you are saying, "I want more money," well, five dollars is more money. I know you are meaning that you want a life free of worrying about how you might take care of your family and meet your financial obligations and have money left over for some fun. I tell you that the first step is getting clear. If you believe it is possible, so shall it be.

What if your intention is to manifest an extra five thousand dollars a month? If this seems too much to manifest, consider an amount that is believable for you. Five hundred, two hundred, even one hundred, it's your choice. Remember: you can have anything you believe is possible. Start where you are, choosing a number that is believable—now is not the time to worry about the 'hows.' Actually, there is never a time to worry about the 'hows.' Let the universe take care of the details. Watch how the universe moves heaven and earth to bring forth the monies you desire. If you are trying to figure it out, you are off the mark. If you are worried about the 'hows', you are off track, and you'll be getting more of the same. Once you are clear about money, move through the formula and manifest your financial desires. Get out of your way and let the universe bring it to you in the most magical way.

Appreciation

Step 2: Appreciate the money you have now. It doesn't matter how much you have or don't have, just appreciate it. This will open the channels for more to come in. Appreciate every little bit that comes to you. This will also begin to shift your feelings about money. The universe doesn't know how much money is in your bank account; it is responding to how you feel about money. By appreciating it you began to change your financial affairs for the better. Give it some time, and you will see that you are the manifester: by your belief, and so it is.

Could you be willing to appreciate more money flowing into your life on a regular basis? Most would want to see the money flowing first before they can appreciate it. This is the reason most have the lives they are living; they look at what is there or not there and focus on it. This is a fine line to walk. If you are focused on not having the money, you will have more of the same experience! If you are looking at the thing in your experience and complaining about it, this too creates the same. I offer you another option: appreciation. Could you appreciate more business, more clients, more students, more sales? I promise you, start where you are and the universe will take care of the rest. Are you willing to appreciate the money you have right now? It doesn't matter how much or how little—just appreciate it! Be sincere, for after all, the universe knows the truth about how you feel.

Don't give up when it doesn't show up on your timetable. What you are doing is shifting your energy around money. I assure you, you will start to relax around money issues if you do this from a place of truth. Do not hesitate to use Words and Affirmations or any of the other steps to stay aligned with your desires. Feel free to imagine things working out. From this moment forward, you get to manifest the financial security you deserve, one conscious step at a time.

Alignment

Step 3: Go to where the money is. Go window shopping at the finest stores. Get magazines of your favorite cars, homes and clothes, like Fortune magazine. Find those around you who are successful. Watch TV programs about wealth. Choose programs that inspire you. There are books on money, wealth and abundance. All will get you into alignment with money. It is up to you what you focus on. Pick and choose the best from what you are observing. Be inspired by all that is abundant. Start by being in a place of trust. If you have done the imagining process, you should have clear images naturally flowing through you. Tune into those images and feel it, see it in as much detail as possible. If you are doing it sincerely, with a light and easy heart, there should also be feelings of hope and joy, a knowing that all is well. If it is more money you are wanting— and it is—you will be inspired to a new thing that will bring you the money you are seeking. Now you are making your decisions from a place of peace, without worry. You move forward, and before long, money is flowing into your life. You will become aligned with new avenues of cash flow, at first, by opening up to the endless possibilities of manifesting.

Energetic Foundation

Step 4: The groundwork has been laid. You are now in a space of confidence, where the outside world does not matter. You see the money, you know it's is en route to you. It is about what you desire to experience, nothing more. Just keep your eye, mind, and heart on the goal—the money you are manifesting. Remain open and at ease and enjoy the magic. Money will begin to flow from unexpected places, all day and in every way.

Expectancy

Step 5: What do you expect to manifest? If you are saying that you believe that the money you are manifesting is on its way, but preparing for its opposite, you will get what you prepare for. If you are needing extra money for bills and are planning what you might say if the money doesn't come, the money will not come. The universe is magnificent in its creation of your desires. It will bring the truth of your expectations. If you know the money is available, then you might have a different attitude. You may be thinking about how wonderful it will feel having the money to pay the bills with money left over. In this feeling space, you are not worried. You are joyful knowing that all is done, and so shall it be! Now what are you expecting?

Words and Affirmations

Step 6: Now is the fun part. Words are a very powerful tool for changing your life. What words could you say to get you closer to manifesting your financial goals? Let's say that you are unsure of the formula thus far and you are not getting it. You could use words fueled with emotions, excitement, and joy to make major changes. You should choose words that resonate with you, that bring about images and feelings of hope. Shifting the way you think about your finances is what must happen first, before you will start to feel better. Talk yourself into success. You must know the power of your words. Take a moment to say something nice to yourself. "Everything is going to work out. It always does." The more you are willing to say something that feels better, the better you will feel. If you are halfheartedly using your words, then your experience must be as it is. You can't pretend with the universe; it knows your heart and the truth behind what you are saying. It knows whether you are believing what you are saying or not, and it will respond accordingly.

You could also say, "Money, comes to me all the time. Money is always on time. I am now more grateful, more thankful for all that I have."

INTENTION

Step 7: What are your intentions, now that you are clear? In this phase you must intend to be open to receiving the money. You must be open to all possibilities as to how it might show up. If you are asked to work late, this could be one of the ways the universe is responding to your request. If this is the case, you should acknowledge the process with a thank you, and keep moving. I assure you, the universe is just getting started. Intend to pay close attention to all the extra money coming into your life after you set your intentions to manifest more cash. Watch for the signs and clues and get happy about this process—make it fun!

IMAGINATION

Step 8: Imagination is having the ability to see a new experience beyond the one you're having. If you are making time on a regular basis to see a new world, it must come. The more you take the time to see what you are wanting to see, you will soon notice the universe responding to the new images you are focused upon. Hasn't this been the case thus far? Use your imagination to see a new life! Let your mind wander to the goodness. It is about making time to think about something that you desire to manifest. Imagine a life free of debt, imagine yourself buying the car, house, clothes, and any and everything you wish to have in your experience. What would you do if you were debt-free? What would you do if you had the extra money in your bank account? The key is being willing to answer these questions as if it is possible. If you are saying, "I can't imagine it!" this would be the reason why you are not debt-free! If you are saying that you are broke then you will not have the extra cash to do the things you desire. Whatever the mind believes, you will soon see it in your experience. The idea that you might say "I can't imagine this or that" is a belief. The thing that gets in the way of imagination is trying to figure out how you might pull it off. It is only your limited belief and lack of imagination that keeps you tied to your present experience. May you use this formula to go beyond all you have imagined before . . . and get out of your own way.

Feeling It

Step 9: You must feel wealthy. Every step is building on the next. If you have done all of the prior steps, you should be feeling the excitement of more money coming. You are now worry-free, thinking about what you might do with this new found wealth. Remember: it is up to you to decide which images you are focused upon. Feel what it will feel like when you have the money in your bank account. Feel what it will feel like when you are paying off your debts. Feel what it will feel like when you can take your dream vacation. Feel what it will feel like when you are in your new house, your new car, boat, etc. If you are wanting a new job that will give you freedom and cash flow, how does it feel? What is the feeling of abundance? Most say it feels like security and freedom. Choose to experience the feelings of security and do the same for financial freedom.

Trust

Step 10: When moving into a space of trust, you move about your business as usual knowing all is well. Once you are in this space, your money worries will be a thing of the past. The key to this process is remembering your desire and seeing what you are manifesting as already in your possession. The universe is responding to the truth of what you are feeling. If you have done these steps as suggested, without moving to the next step until you have mastered the prior one, you know the necessity of feeling it. You can't dupe the universe by pretending. After all we are spiritual beings having a physical experience. We can pretend to one another, and some may fall for it, but the universe won't. There are no secrets with the universe; it gives you the truth whether you are aware of it or not. Put another way, if you offer baloney, guess what you will be eating sooner or later! In moments of the formula you are asked to fake it, to conjure up feelings of truth in the moment so you might offer something new in the way you are feeling to the universe. In that moment, the universe is unaware if it is really in your experience. It is giving you your feeling of the thing.

Surrender

Step 11: By now the question should be "What money?" When you are in complete surrender, you live your life and all that you need shows up effortlessly. Money is a necessity, and the moment you trust in yourself and the undeniable connection you have with the things that are showing up in your life, the better off you will be, the better off the world will be! You truly are the manifester! When you fully embrace this idea, you are no longer concerned about how it will come and continue to come.

You should be free of your money worries. Use the formula until you have a new attitude about money. Keep in mind that it is up to you and what you are willing to let in by taking time to work the formula. Surrender is another way of saying "I'm not going to try and figure out the details." If you feel inspired to do something out of excitement, then this is inspired action, which is a huge difference from acting out of fear. Acting out of fear will usually take you on a wild goose chase with all sorts of hurdles in your way. Because you're trying to figure it out, you do not have a clear picture of the unlimited potential for money to come into your life.

Everything you desire can be obtained by using this formula. Reread the stories and see which steps are being used. You could look to your own manifestations and see which steps you've used or are using. Now you have a clear-cut path to your desires. No one is responsible for what you choose to focus on. You may tune into energies on a regular basis that may manifest something similar in your experience. If you are not making a conscious effort to think a new thought the things you are focused on will become your experience, your life. You have the freedom to manifest the best you can imagine.

Manifesting Process for Well-Being

Clarity

Step 1: Well-being applies to all aspects of life: when you think of well-being what does it mean? What do you desire to experience? If you were living a life of well-being, what would you do on a daily basis? How is it different than what you are doing now?

Would you listen to your body? Would you honor yourself? Would you choose a harmonious lifestyle? Would you do things that bring you joy? Would you take the time to get to know yourself? Would you spend time with yourself? Would you choose well-being in every aspect of your life? The ideas of honor and alignment come to mind. As I choose peace, I am choosing well-being.

As I choose love, I am choosing well being. As I am putting myself first, so I might have a chance to be the shining light for those around me. I desire to be the picture of well-being in all my affairs. My thoughts must be focused on well-being and followed by my words and actions.

Appreciation

Step 2: I tell you this, when I am not feeling well, I wish for well-being. I appreciate feeling healthy, vibrant, and energized. I am not wanting to manifest such an experience that I may appreciate well-being. I am being in appreciation on a daily basis for all the wonder flowing through my body and giving thanks regularly. If I am doing what I love, I am appreciating well-being. When I am listening to myself, I am appreciating well-being. When I am loving myself, I am appreciating well-being, and I get more of it.

Alignment

Step 3: This means doing whatever it takes to align yourself with well-being. Starting with the way you think and what you give your attention to, align your thoughts with well-being. Find words and affirmations to help with this process. It is possible! You must be willing to try something new. I offer thoughts as the first things that must change, because soon after your experience will start to shift. You are now sowing new seeds of well-being.

Energetic Foundation

Step 4: Are you energized by your desire for well-being? Are you confident? Are you moving forward, offering thoughts and ideas aligned with your ideal end result? When you fully embrace this step, you move into a space of knowing. In this space, no is not an option. You are inspired by new ideas and images that confirm that you are on the path to well-being. The more you tune into this energy, the more you experience the feelings of complete harmony, balance, and of course, well-being.

Expectancy

Step 5: Are you expecting a full recovery? Are you expecting everything to go well? This concept applies to every aspect of your life. The thing is, when you are well-being, all is wonderful. If the universe is indeed responding to your energy, then it must give you the life level that you are offering. Take a moment to look at your life and at what you are experiencing right now. How has your thinking played a part in what you see before you? If you are honest, you will see that it is the same. If you feel that life is hard, then it will be. If you feel that life is a blessing, you will experience it as such. I want you to know once and for all that you have the power. You are the power. Now use it to experience well-being.

Words and Affirmations

Step 6: I believe we can change our life by changing our words. What we talk about, worry about, complain about, gossip about . . . all is creative. Listen to yourself and the words you choose to describe your life. As you are noticing your world and making judgments, you will find yourself in similar situations. By your words are you justified or condemned. Most people are not aware of the power they possess. They use words like "can't," "hard," "barely getting by." Sometimes people say, "I am a bit under the weather"—what are you doing "under there" anyway? "I feel a cold coming on"—isn't that an invitation? Even if you are saying you're not going to get it, that is an invitation too. Instead, notice what you talk about, say "I feel wonderful," and the body will follow your belief. You are constantly sowing seeds with your words. If you hear something long enough, you may start to believe it. Truthfully, most do believe the misguided information, never taking time to investigate where these opinions came from. Let today be the day for change. Use your words to create a life worth living.

Intention

Step 7: Is it your intention to do something nice for yourself on a daily basis? If you are choosing to exercise on a daily basis, you are demonstrating your intention to stay on the path to well-being. If your intention is to read an inspiring book, or to choose foods that are nutritious and light, this also keeps you on your path to well-being. Are you intending to live a life of peace, joy, abundance, love and humility? If this is your desire, then you should be aware of the choices you make by intending it, then you might truly reside in a space for well-being.

Imagination

Step 8: What does well-being look like? Where do you see yourself in regard to well-being? How about this: do you wish to be the healing power, the power of complete acceptance and love? This energy is flowing through you to remind you that you are well-being. Well-being is the fullness of all you desire, in every aspect of your life, mind, body, and soul. If it is physical change that you desire to experience, take time to envision your ideal state.

For example, let's take a disease that you are wanting to release. What is the best you can imagine when you think of your new and healed self? Remember, you are the manifester. This may be a hard pill to swallow. If you are the manifester, then it's safe to say you manifested your present state of affairs. The good news is that you can now imagine something better! It is flowing through you, this amazing manifesting power. Nothing is happening to you.

Feeling It

Step 9: The world is perfect and so are we. It is the illusion of inharmonious thinking that keeps us chained to unhappy circumstances. We have the power and the freedom to use it however we choose… the trick is remembering that we have all we need to live the life of our dreams. What does well-being feel like if you are not sure what could it feel like, if all is well?

If you are fulfilled in all your desires, what would you be doing if you were in a state of well-being? One might say, "I wish to travel the world. I would do all I want, when I am wanting to do it." That's a great start. You must start somewhere. I am sure that once you have done all you believe you would in a state of well-being, there would be more to do. My guess is that you might want to be of service to others. I've noticed that most people I've met do wish to be of service in some way, giving back. When you are in a state of well-being, it might be a natural response to share and to be of service. If you wish to experience it, what does it feel like to have the capacity to travel the world? How would it feel to do what you are wanting, when you are wanting to do it?

If you are being easy and willing to play a bit, you can conjure up such feelings. Actors do it all the time. After all, the world is but a stage! Why not pretend to experience what you wish to manifest? I assure you that you have acted out this life level. If you are not in the best physical condition, you must act like someone who doesn't care much about well-being. This may have a lot to do with the life you are living. If you are saying, "I do all the right things," what about the thoughts you are thinking? Do you understand that the universe is the perfect matchmaker, bringing the exact thoughts you're thinking to your door via your experiences, your life? Sometimes this energy is made manifest in your physical body.

Trust

Step 10: Do you trust that all is well? If you answered yes, do you act as if all is well? If you are wanting to change a physical condition from one of illness to one of well-being, you must trust that your prayers and desires have been answered. When you are trusting, your attitude changes. You think differently, you see what you desire to experience. Remember: act as if! There is no room for doubt, no buts, just the well-being you desire. Now is the time to be at peace and listen for divine guidance. The universe will inspire you to new heights, a new life, a new belief as to what is possible. And so shall it be.

Sʼurrender

Step 11: Once you have the clear image of well-being in every aspect of your life, surrender it. The universe will take care of the details. There are too many ways in which the universe may deliver you to the life you are manifesting. Trust the universe—it has great taste! It must be similar to what you are wanting, or even better. We can't see the big picture, but it is always much more then we've imagined. Once you surrender, pay close attention to the signs. Everything is potentially a sign, if you are open to seeing it. This doesn't mean that you are searching for them, but if you are in a place of surrender, they reveal themselves to you. It is that simple. It is happening anyway, but now you are consciously participating in manifesting the life you say you wish to live.

Manifesting Process for Joy

CLARITY

Step 1: What is joy? What does joy mean to you? Get clear about the things that bring forth joy. Look around at your immediate experience and notice things that might be joyous. Be playful when you are thinking of joyous things to do. Come up with ideas around joy, things that are joyous to you. Reading a good book may be joyous, going on nature walks or spending time with friends and family. This is something you must give serious consideration. It is anything that puts you at ease, feeling joyous to participate in an activity. You know what makes you feel good, something that brings about a feeling of joy.

APPRECIATION

Step 2: Notice joyous things you could appreciate. Find images of joy and appreciate them. If going on vacation will bring about joy, appreciate it all day long. In every moment, choose to find something joyous to appreciate. As you see others having fun doing what they love and being in the moment, lighten up! Take time to appreciate the freedom someone may be experiencing, and it will then tune you into feeling joy just by your willingness to notice it.

The day will be the day; it is always up to you to decide what to do with it. You have the freedom to either appreciate it or find yourself preoccupied with everything but joy. If your intention is to experience joy, it will make itself known in every moment, regardless of what the weather is doing.

Alignment

Step 3: What are some ways you could get into alignment with joy? I think the most important thing is to do something different. If you have made a list, choose one thing to experience, and do it. If you are believing that you can't or are unsure of where to start, just imagine what you would do if you were given three wishes. Try it for yourself! The more you are willing to think joyous thoughts, the easier it will be when you are wanting to align with joy. If leaving work on time brings you joy, do it! If sleeping in on Mondays brings you joy, do it! If taking a walk on the beach on your lunch break brings you joy, do it! If sitting at home on Friday night reading an inspiring book brings you joy, do it! What are you willing to do to experience joy? Once you decide what you are willing to do, do it!

Energetic Foundation

Step 4: Now what does this have to do with joy? I believe that once you have your mind set on manifesting something, it becomes more real. Once you have focused long enough or talked about it until you are in a place of knowingness, there is nothing anyone can say to shift your desires. Energetic foundation is the excitement of experiencing joy. It's the possibility of your desire made manifest. The more you can tune into joy, dreaming, hoping, wishing, and praying for the full experience of it, without a doubt, you are sure to be standing on solid ground. Now watch the magic unfold. The bottom line is that you cannot be moved by anything that may be a contradiction to your desires and beliefs.

Expectancy

Step 5: What are you expecting? You have all that you have expected up until this point in your life. Are you walking the talk? What a concept! Isn't everyone walking the talk? If you are living a life of inharmonious experiences or harmonious, joyous experiences, you are expecting one or the other. That's simple enough. It takes a little time and practice to choose joy and expect it. The idea that you get what you expect must be understood on a deeper level. When you get this, you will begin to expect something new, something better.

Words and Affirmations

Step 6: You could use words to feel better and slowly move towards joy. Choose words like excitement, ecstatic, pleasure, satisfaction, delight, contentment, happiness, bliss—words that bring about good feelings. Your intention to experience joy will infuse your words and be backed by emotions and feelings. If you say it enough, you will start to believe it. In the same way, if you listen to negative words often enough, you will begin to believe them. "I can never do anything right," "Life is an uphill battle," "I'm not good enough!" These defeating words and phrases, when reiterated on a daily basis, thus becoming common place for an insecure person seeking approval. Before long, you begin to believe the opinions of others, you adopt these ideas as self-talk and self-perception. As you make time to reflect on your experience as a child, which words come to mind? Which names were you called? What were some negative opinions of you that you may have heard growing up? When you were called a negative name, it didn't make you feel good about yourself; as a child, you may have believed it. Let that be all the proof you will ever need. Take time to listen to the words you say to yourself, and consider where they came from.

Now looking back, doesn't it make sense to let go of these useless words and phrases? What if someone called you a car. Would you be a car, could you be a car? You could not. Even if you wanted to please this person, it's not possible! When you love and accept yourself completely, there is no way you can be anything but that which you were created: PURE LOVE. This is the truth of who you are.

INTENTION

Step 7: Is it your intention to experience joy? I hear people say yes to this question more times than I care to admit. The truth of the matter is that you can't experience joy if you are focused on things that do not bring about joyous feelings. I listen to some topics they choose to engage in, the negative TV programs they watch in the name of entertainment. It is up to you to determine which feelings are evoked by the things you are choosing to focus on. If you are intending to experience joy, then you must understand that all you are tuned into is bringing about emotions and feelings, so it is in your best interest to set your intention to find joy in all you are doing, observing, and sharing.

Is it your intention to be joyful? Do you intend to spread joy? Are you a joyous person? What do you intend on a daily basis? I tell you this, if you have not set your intention, you will have more of the same. Usually you call forth things from your previous experience by default because you're on automatic; you're not making a conscious decision to be something different, something more. May your new desire to experience more joy be at the forefront of your mind as you intend a joyful life, relationship, marriage, work place and family. The act of intending something puts you in the driver's seat with all the responsibility in your hands.

Such phrases comes to mind: Debbie Downer, the bearer of bad news, killjoy, etc . . . if you know someone like this, pay attention to your mood before and after your experience with that person. Be aware of what you are sharing you could be this person. What do you think you bring to your friendships, your work environment, your family? Are you choosing to inspire and uplift your friends and coworkers and the world? What are you leaving behind energetically?

Imagination

Step 8: What thoughts come to mind when you think of joy? The great thing about your imagination is that you can go anywhere your mind will take you. If you can imagine it, then it is possible. If this is a bit of a challenge, then what could you be joyous for? Look out in the world and find it. Ask and you shall receive. Your intention is to manifest joy, to experience more joy in your life. There are all sorts of things that may put you in a joyous mood. Doing something nice for someone, walking your dog, sitting in the park, people watching, spending time with an old friend, volunteering, helping a friend in need, participating in a class that stimulates your creative mind… all of these things could be joyous.

If you are asking the question, "What brings me joy?," I promise that you will get an image or an idea. Remember: all you need is within, even the answer to what brings you joy. It's about asking the right question.

Feeling It

Step 9: Once you know what brings you joy, the feeling of it should be easy. It starts in your mind, your thoughts, with thinking thoughts of joy and using your words at every opportunity to share joy. When someone asks you how you are, what can you say? If everything is changing, wouldn't it be truthful to say that things are getting better? If you are familiar with the law of attraction, choosing to focus on the joy will bring forth the joy.

Consider saying, "I'm wonderful!," and before long you will be—if you believe it! If you repeat inspiring words long enough, you will conjure the feelings to support them. This will be the case when you are committed to change. The universe will always meet you where you are.

Trust

Step10: Do you trust that life can be joyful? With a little participation on your part, I assure you that it will be at your fingertips. Do you trust that joy is within your grasp if you truly desire it? Do you trust that nature is a great example of joyousness, how the leaves dance in the wind while rejoicing in the sun? Have you noticed the joy of your pets? I love watching dogs meeting one another out on a leisurely walk with their owners, who may or may not have spoken to each other otherwise. The excitement is wonderful! They immediately go into play mode. I've also notice dogs who couldn't be bothered and others that were not so friendly, but I'm not talking about them. I'm choosing to talk about the dogs that get so excited to see another dog, it's as if they are seeing a long lost friend. I often wonder, what are they thinking? Are they not true examples of unconditional love and joy? If you wish to experience joy, look around—it's everywhere!

Surrender

Step11: This might seem a little tricky. If joy is a state of being, a feeling, an emotion, how could you surrender it? What if you are waiting to go on vacation, and this is the joy you are seeking, is this something you could surrender? You can do the same thing for the feeling of joy. I think setting the intention and releasing it, knowing that you will soon start to feel more joy, is a great start. No worries—know that all will work out just fine. Put your attention on a thing long enough, and the universe must show you signs of what you've been focused on. Let your life be the example, the lesson from which to draw wisdom and resolution.

part three
Affirmations

I Am The Manifester

Affirmations for Love

Love is clear when I am loving towards myself.

I intend to be more loving.

I appreciate myself in more loving ways.

I am energized by loving thoughts.

I expect to love the way I desire to be loved.

I am aligned with unconditional love.

I am using my words and affirmations
to experience more love.

I imagine the feeling of love flowing through me
accepting me as I am.

I am feeling more love for life.

Affirmations for Love

I am trusting love, as I am love.

I surrender to love.

Love is the truth of my being.

I see the world through the eyes of love.

Love is my natural state.

In every breath I am taking the opportunity to experience love.

My life is filled with love.

Love follows me day and night, healing all my affairs.

Love is the best option.

When I am loving, love is enough.

I Am The Manifester

Affirmations for Joy

I am joyous and I now experience a fulfilling life.

I intend to experience joy on a daily basis.

I am appreciating joy in every moment.

I am joyous and energetic.

I expect to be joyous.

I am aligned with joy and I experience it daily.

I am using my words and affirmations to manifest more joy in my world.

I am imagining my world filled with joy.

I feel joyous just because.

I am trusting my joyful feeling.

Affirmations for Joy

I joyfully trust.

My journey is joyous.

I choose joy on a daily basis.

I am joyful.

Joy is the way.

I am joyous and the world
responds in kind.

When I am joyous, I encounter joyful people.

Joy open doors to opportunities unforeseen.

Joy is the key to endless possibilities.

I Am The Manifester

Affirmations for Peace

Peace is my only choice.

I am at peace as I move through my world.

I choose to notice things in the world
that inspire peaceful feelings.

I offer peace to all I encounter.

I am peaceful as peace flows freely in all my affairs,
resolving them in peaceful ways.

I am at peace all day, every day.

Peace starts with a choice to be peaceful.

I am peaceful from the inside out.

When I am peaceful, so too is my world.

When I am looking for peace I always find it.

Affirmations for Peace

I experience peace daily.

I am peaceful.

I am at peace in all my affairs.

My desire for peace is a reality.

My thoughts are of peace.

I am always looking for peaceful solutions.

Peace is the path to right action.

When I am peaceful, I notice peace in the world.

Peace opens my heart to well-being.

Great ideas flow freely through my peaceful heart.

I intend peace, and so shall it be.

When I am peaceful, there is nothing to prove.

I Am The Manifester

AFFIRMATIONS FOR WELL-BEING

I intend to experience well-being in all my affairs.

I am appreciating all that is going well in my world.

I am energized by my desires for well-being.

I expect well-being, and therefore all is well.

I am now aligned with well-being in my
thoughts, words, and deeds.

I am now using my words and affirmations
to manifest a life of well-being.

I am imagining a life of well-being.

I am well-being in every moment.

I am trusting that all is well

Affirmations for Well-Being

I look for well-being in my world.

I now let go and trust that all is well.

I am willing to heal my life by healing myself.

I am well-being, myself.

I expect well-being.

I am in tune with thoughts of well-being.

I am well-being manifested.

Well-being is my natural state.

When I am well-being, all is well in my word.

All is well when I am just being.

I Am The Manifester

Affirmations for Abundance

The world is constantly giving me my desires.

I have all I could ever need in this moment,
as I am abundant in all thy ways.

I am all I am meant to be in every area of my life.

Abundance flows through me to my heart's desires.

I appreciate what I have, and where I am,
abundance flows naturally.

Abundance is self-worth manifested.

I am abundant in all my affairs under grace.

I tune into abundant ideas flowing day and night,
and all is right in my world.

Abundance is seeking me all day, every day, in every way.

When I am appreciating abundance,
it is always available.

Affirmaitons for Abundance

I am abundance flowing freely, bringing forth
all my desires.

I am abundant, and so it is.

My natural state of being is abundance.

I am more abundant today in every possible way.

I am abundance in the flesh, giving and receiving.

Abundance always follow great ideas.

Abundance flows through me, to me, for me.

I am the abundance overflowing in my world.

My thoughts are focused on abundance,
day in and day out.

I see only abundance in all I encounter.

I feel the flow of abundance in
every aspect of my life.

I Am The Manifester

Affirmations for Money

I am clear that money flows freely to me daily.

I intend to have more money than I need.

I appreciate money and use it wisely.

Money is energy flowing towards good vibrations.

I expect to have money for all I desire, and so it is.

I see money coming quickly, under grace,
from every possible place.

I imagine money flowing, growing, and flowing to me
through me for my greater good.

I feel secure knowing that I have all the money I need,
and then some.

I surrender to the flow of money coming fast, fast, fast.

Money flows freely and effortlessly to me daily.

Affirmations for Money

I have more money than I can spend.

I have the money I need today in a timely way, under grace.

Money follows me all day, every day, ready to play.

There is always more money to spend for all that is great.

I use money wisely for the goodness of all concerned.

Money loves to be shared.

I love sharing money, it keeps coming and coming.

Money is my trusted friend, it is always on time.

I use money for fun in the sun.

I love doing great things with money.

I use money to help others.

When I love what I do, money comes easily, daily.

Big quick cash comes fast, fast, fast.

Affirmations for Forgiveness

I forgive and I feel better.

The more I forgive, the better I feel.

I forgive, so I might live a life of emotional freedom.

Forgiveness is the gift I give to myself.

I forgive to create a new experience.

Forgiveness is waiting to be embraced.

Forgiveness is letting go.

I forgive myself for not forgiving you.

I forgive to be free.

Forgiveness allows me to love.

Affirmations for Forgiveness

Forgiveness inspires me to live.

I forgive to experience more love.

I forgive you completely and freely.

I am willing to forgive.

I forgive you.

Love is about forgiving.

I forgive to move forward.

I forgive you as life forgive me.

Forgiveness begins with myself.

I forgive you and wish you well.

Forgiveness is easy.

Forgiveness is a choice.

I Am The Manifester

Affirmations for Appreciation

I see my home as it is, and appreciate all I have.

I appreciate my body just because,
and I experience beauty and wellness.

As I appreciate my life,
there is always more to appreciate.

I appreciate money, and money appreciates me
and flows to me daily.

When I appreciate my work I find my fulfillment.

I appreciate my relationships by seeing the goodness in my lover.

I appreciate this moment as it is
and give birth to something wonderful.

I appreciate my life right here, right now.

I appreciate myself just as I am.

Affirmations for Appreciation

I appreciate life and all it has to offer.

I am appreciating great health.

I am appreciating my family and friends.

I am appreciating the process.

I am appreciating the end result.

I am appreciating all parties concerned.

I appreciate life to experience beauty.

Appreciation puts me on the right path.

I am appreciating life for all I desire.

I appreciate life and I appreciate you.

Appreciation aligns me with right ideas.

I appreciate life just as it is.

I appreciate you now and forever.

About the Author

Tobi Ellison was an inquisitive child who asked important questions.
"Where did I come from?"
"Why am I here?"
"What is my purpose?"

"Ask and you shall receive."
Tobi Ellison is a truth seeker who, through years of trial and error, discovered we are more connected to the universe than once thought. He now believes the universe is flowing through us and that nothing is happening to us. We are the manifesters of our lives, our experiences! He says we have the life we are dreaming about or complaining about, no more, no less. It is up to each individual to discover this truth for themselves.

Tobi Ellison is a Spiritual Advisor, Reiki Master, Spiritual Life Coach and Manifesting Coach.

He currently lives in Los Angeles, California where he teaches these truths and reminds those he encounters to manifest the life of their dreams by telling a new story, the one in which they wish to experience.

www.ingramcontent.com/pod-product-compliance
Lightning Source LLC
Chambersburg PA
CBHW061759110426
42742CB00012BB/2193